Praise for Alan Scott's

THE QUEST FOR VIRTUE

Delightfully humorous, painfully honest and always spiritually centered, Alan Scott's *The Quest for Virtue* will lift you up and help you in times of need.
– *Laurie Hill Crosbie, M.A., author of Salvation In Indiana*

Alan Scott is that rare kind of writer that seeks to grow in virtue by honestly confronting our most common vices and distractions. He doesn't shy away from the struggle of everyday life, instead recognizing great potential for growth, even during our mundane or often frustrating days. If you want to start cultivating the habits of true virtue, his practical advice and words of wisdom in *The Quest for Virtue* is the perfect place to start.
– *Michael J. Lichens, editor and host of Catholic Exchange*

Quest for Virtue is a wonderfully written-testimony of the goodness, faithfulness, and mercy of God. It is a poignant reminder that when we allow ourselves to "be still and know that I am God", He can and will work in and through our lives. The writer echoes the words of St. Augustine's cry; my heart will not rest, O God, until it rests in you.
– *Br. Boltoph, O/OSB, The Order of St. Benedict, Servants of Jesus Bethlehem Priory*

In a world full of vice, Alan Scott shares the necessary tools with the reader to live a life of virtue. If you desire to become a happier and holier person, this book holds the road map to success.
– *Fr. Edward Looney, author of A Rosary Litany*

Grab *The Quest for Virtue* next time you're stressed, worried, discouraged… or about to strangle someone. Its gentle wisdom and humor will ease you back to sanity, back to the person you know you can be. Alan doesn't trumpet maxims from the mountaintop – he's struggling right there with you, but maybe a few steps ahead. This collection of essays provides guidance to those new to the spiritual journey and encouragement for those who've been on it for a while. Either way, pack this book as a trusty companion.
– *Rose Folsom, author of VirtueConnection.com*

The Quest for Virtue offers simple yet profound reminders of how we might better focus on God. Pleasant to read and insightful, Alan Scott addresses issues mothers face on a daily basis: distractions, living in the present, and patience. He presents a challenge to all aspiring saints, and every mother desiring to grow in virtue in the midst of family life.
– *Denise Renner, author of The Motherlands*

The virtue of Alan Scott's *The Quest for Virtue: A Journey to Union with God* lies in its simplicity, simplicity itself being one of the virtues he addresses that can best help us focus on things that truly matter the most – God and the things of God, including the right relations to ourselves and our neighbors. *The Quest for Virtue* is an accessible, reliable, and enjoyable guide on that journey toward God through virtue. It teems with humor, the author's heartfelt life lessons, common sense, and not-so-common insights on how to practice every day the kinds of behaviors that lead to all sorts of good and Godly habits of thinking, feeling, and doing that are the stuff of the virtues.
– *Kevin Vost, Psy.D., author of The One-Minute Aquinas*

"Virtue" has disappeared from public conversation, and it's fading from discussion even in the Protestant Christian circles in which I travel. It's time we decided to grow in virtue again, with Christ at the center of our hope and striving. Both practical and spiritual in its approach, Alan Scott's book is a timely and helpful guide and reminder to Grow in Virtue.
– *Tom Gilson, Senior Editor and Ministry Coordinator, The Stream; Editor, True Reason: Confronting the Irrationality of the New Atheism*

Everyone is seeking happiness but often times in the wrong places. Consumerism, individualism and relativism has in many ways taken over our culture and keeps joy and our sense of purpose far from our reach. Alan Scott gives readers simple and practical solutions to this epidemic by connecting with the reader and bringing to light common interior struggles that we all experience but rarely discuss. "The Quest for Virtue" with its honesty, thoughtful format and easy-to-read style, is the perfect resource for experiencing the joy and peace of leading a life of simplicity, virtue and union with God.
- *Sheena E. Lukose, author of The Pelican Box*

THE QUEST FOR VIRTUE

A JOURNEY TO UNION WITH GOD

ALAN SCOTT

Ordering Information:
Quantity sales. Special discounts are available on quantity
purchases by corporations, associations and others.
For details, contact the publisher at the email address below.

Orders by U.S. trade bookstores and wholesalers. Please contact
us at info@growinvirtue.com or visit www.growinvirtue.com.
Printed in the United States of America.

ISBN: 978-0-692-94844-6

This book is dedicated to the memory of my mother Margaret Rose, who supported my writing and was always asking me when this book would be ready. It's ready mom!

CONTENTS

FOREWORD

So, let's just cut to the chase. What is virtue, and why is it so important?

Well, I can tell you that the Catechism of the Catholic Church defines human virtue as "firm attitudes, stable dispositions, habitual perfections of intellect and will that govern our actions, order our passions and guide our conduct according to reason and faith." [1]

Additionally, I believe virtues are singular, hard-earned graces provided to us by God, through our diligence and love for God, that fill our soul, making us better people, who demonstrate "morally good behavior or character," [2] out of a deep and sincere love for God.

And as we work hard to strengthen each virtue, our soul is penetrated, and becomes more aligned to the goodness of God and His will.

This book is conceived from the website, GrowInVirtue.com, where I have written about many topics concerning virtue, ranging from patience to charity, to even preparing for one's own death.

The intent of the Grow in Virtue blog has always been to take each of its readers on a journey towards a life filled with more virtue, faith, simplicity, generosity, and far less complexity.

A journey to union with God.

Since starting Grow in Virtue, many of its readers have suggested that I collect the most popular and inspiring articles from the blog and organize them into book form, for easy reference.

So, this book *The Quest for Virtue* is just that – a collection of the most relevant blog articles from the website, divided into seven different themes, each edited and organized into an order that provides the reader with an appreciably different experience from reading the

[1] *Catechism of the Catholic Church, Part Three, Life of Christ, Article 7, The Virtues*
[2] *Merriam-Webster*

articles independently online. It also includes some new material, not previously published on the Grow in Virtue site.

Please note that each of these articles are individual topics. While I organized this material in a deliberate and thoughtful manner, it is not meant to function as a linear narrative; rather, it is meant to serve as a dialogue between me, the author, and you, the reader.

Every chapter is a single, stand-alone topic. My goal is to provide you with many important topics on virtue, relayed in a simple, easy-to-read style, so that you may construct your own guide for creating a life that is filled with more virtue, happiness and a sincere love for God.

Many of these chapters include moments from my life, yet they are the personal joys and struggles that we all seem to have in common. I wrote this book with the sole hope and purpose to challenge and inspire you.

Oh yes, I almost forgot to answer why virtue is so important ...

A LITTLE THING CALLED PERSPECTIVE

Near-death accidents.

Self-reflection.

Priorities.

What do they all have in common? Well, at least for me, they helped me to gain some much-needed perspective.

April 14, 2010 is a day that I will never forget.

Having made an, "it's about time," exit from winter, spring was amongst us. And the grass in my lawn was screaming, "Alan, give me a haircut!"

With no gas in my shed to show for, I decided to head over to the nearest gas station. So, my friend Matt and I jumped into my car and headed out.

But my grass wasn't mowed that day. And we never made it to the gas station.

What did happen that day? I ended up with seven broken ribs, a punctured lung, a fractured spine and a severed spleen.

You see, on the way to getting the gas, a man driving a tractor-trailer was a bit impatient, went through a red light and subsequently ran into my car going about 70 miles per hour.

My car didn't survive that day, but, miraculously, both my friend Matt and I did.

It was a near-death accident.

We lived.

Barely.

Actually, we survived by about a second, according to the police officer who came to visit me in the hospital. The tractor-trailer hit the front of my car, spinning us several times into a nearby ravine. Another second, he would have hit me dead-on at my driver's side door, which would have killed us both instantly.

I didn't see the tractor-trailer coming and was yelling out with fear, having no idea what was going on.

My car finally stopped spinning from the force of hitting a fence at the bottom of a shallow ditch. I remember clearly thinking, although I had difficulty breathing, "Thank you God, I'm alive."

I also thought, "I'm in some serious pain. I think I'll just rest here until the ambulance arrives."

No such luck.

My friend Matt who was sitting in the passenger seat informed me that the entire hood of my car was on fire … and that we had better get out. Quickly.

So, we did.

Even though I was beat up badly, I managed the energy to eject my seat belt, open my door … and run for about 20 feet, before passing out.

And within less than a minute, (or so I've been told) my entire car was engulfed in flames.

I remember being placed into the ambulance on a backboard, with my head and feet strapped down. I had no idea what had happened to Matt but the ambulance driver told me that he would be OK.

But I wasn't so sure about myself. I couldn't breathe and was gasping for air. I didn't know my left lung was punctured and I thought I was choking to death. I also couldn't move my legs because they were strapped down, and I heard one of the paramedics talking about how I might have broken my spine.

I was terrified. And I was praying to God for help.

And then it happened. As my ambulance started to pull away from the accident scene, we were struck. A car hit our ambulance. One of the paramedics went flying across the back of the ambulance. Another nearly fell on top of me.

And me, barely able to catch my own breath, managed to whisper slowly, and just loud enough to be heard, "Good grief, in the span of 15 minutes, I've been in two car accidents."

Both paramedics laughed. So did I.

At least on the inside.

The second accident was not major (just a dent I was later told), and we proceeded on to the hospital where I received a one-week, all-inclusive stay.

And after being taken care of by a wonderful staff of kind and caring doctors and nurses, I went home to heal.

I rested at home for four weeks before returning to work. According to the doctors, I should have been out of work for at least three months – and they could not believe how quickly I recovered.

I remember the four weeks feeling like an eternity. I was used to being constantly busy, and the downtime gave me a lot of time to think. A lot of time to pray. A lot of time to reflect. Especially about my life.

Since the accident, I have seriously considered my pre-accident priorities, which I'm now sad to admit, were a bit materialistic and shallow.

Talk about gaining perspective. My priorities included working my way up at my corporate job, owning lots of nice things, and well, living mostly for … me.

Since the accident, prayer and self-reflection have helped me to see that I was wasting time and opportunities.

It also has helped me to stop worrying about all my little problems and to start to recognize opportunities to give of myself to others.

It's always hard for me to explain but it's as if God allowed (even willed) the accident, so I could finally see my distorted view of what I perceived as "normal", so God could create a new normal for me.

In the months and years since my near-death accident, I began to realize certain truths, all from God:

1. Most of the small problems that we deal with in life aren't important at all.

2. Our time on earth is short and we should try our best to live it for God, not ourselves.

3. We should focus on living in the present, let go of the past and stop worrying about the future.

About two years after the accident, I left corporate America. I now make far less money, and I'm exponentially happier.

I stopped chasing trends and status purchases and donated a lot of the things I already owned. I started becoming grateful for what I had, versus striving to acquire that which I didn't have.

And most important, I have developed a much stronger relationship with God and it is growing every day, because I am trying to love Him more than myself.

At the end of each day, I now have a routine to express my gratitude to God for three things specific to that day.

But there is one thing that I thank God for each and every day: seven broken ribs, a punctured lung, a fractured spine and a severed spleen.

Preparation for a Closer Relationship with God

WHERE YOUR TREASURE IS, THERE WILL YOUR HEART BE ALSO

For years I lived a life that wasn't very healthy.

I'm not talking about bad food and little exercise. I mean, sure, there was that, but that's wasn't it.

What I am talking about is that I was leading a life that wasn't very conducive to maintaining a healthy soul.

A good comparison we can use is like consuming unhealthy food and drink. When we tend to over-indulge in too much red meat, too much sugar or too much alcohol, the negative side-effects creep up on us and, soon enough, start to take their toll.

Likewise, other things we put into our minds and into our hearts also tend to take their toll on our interior.

These are "treasures" that are not real treasures.

We basically become what we consume on a daily basis.

In the same way that we tend to become unhealthy, if we eat too much unhealthy food, it is also true in regards to the shows we watch, the books we read, the music we listen to, and the internet we often spend countless hours on. Our supposed "treasures".

Each of these things, often without our direct knowledge, will begin to shape our minds and our hearts.

And this is very important.

Perhaps, just as we often in life make a decision to eat healthier foods or go for a walk more often, maybe we should also take a time out to determine if what we're feeding ourselves on a daily basis - the non-food type of consuming - is what is best for us.

Does playing video games for hours each day serve us well?

Does spending over an hour each day reading status updates on our social media accounts help us to be better people?

Does watching and reading the mainstream news create negativity in our lives without our permission?

Does caring about which celebrity is dating which other celebrity do anything to improve our lives?

I can't answer those questions for you but I can speak from my personal experience.

Over ten years ago when I moved into my current home, and because I spent so much time in front of the television in my previous apartment, I decided for my new life – no more television. After a couple of months without it, a surprised friend of mine asked me if I missed watching TV.

And the answer was no.

I realized my life had drastically improved without it. Instead of staring at a box all morning and evening, watching shows that had no positive impact on my life, I was actually doing things that did have a positive impact.

I was reading more. I was spending time with friends and family. I was outside planting a garden. I was learning more about my faith.

I was living.

And broadcast television has never made an appearance back into my home since. I also unsubscribed to many of the magazines I was receiving, especially those filled with news (world and entertainment) and those that promoted superficiality.

I stopped caring about trends – what other people thought was important and started caring about what was good for me.

I developed a 'less-is-more' way of thinking.

And with all these time-consuming things now removed from my life, I have attempted to give more time to things that really matter, especially my relationship with God.

Now, with that said, that doesn't mean I have given my heart perfectly over to things that truly matter. I'm still a work in progress.

I fully admit I allow too much social media into my life.

And I'm not exactly sure why. Unless finding out what burger my friend had for lunch (and snapped a picture of it, too) is somehow beneficial to my life.

But I am working on this. I'm purposely spending far less time on social media. And as for all the other social this-or-that apps out there, I have made a promise to myself to never start using them.

But everyone is different.

Some people may not even use social media or are great at limiting themselves to only perusing social sites for a few minutes a day.

Each person must ask himself or herself, what am I giving my time to? My heart to? My soul to?

And the most important part of this evaluation – you need to be honest with yourself.

As human beings, we were created to worship. Everyone has chosen his own path. Those who choose to worship God give their hearts to Him and let everything else take a second, third, etc., place. Those who choose not to worship God will worship something – always. It could be their car, sports, a person, a pet – the list goes on.

Where your treasure is, there will your heart be also. What are you giving your heart to?

If you immediately start to defend the time you spend on certain aspects of your life, the exercise is futile. Just as I was initially defensive when I was asked if I watched too much television or read too many entertainment magazines.

You must go deep into your heart for the answer.

And by doing this, you can bring positive changes into your life that you never imagined, or even thought possible.

REMOVING DISTRACTIONS

Sometimes I have often felt like I need to let go of 'the world.' There are way too many distractions.

So, I have been abandoning lots of things that used to be very important to me and adopting a whole new way of thinking and a whole new way of being.

I have slowly been moving towards what is called a 'minimalist.' It's funny – I had no intentions to become minimal. My life seemed to be going OK as a 'maximalist.' I had loads of stuff and was quite happy with it, or so I thought.

I discovered the concept of minimalism accidentally, stumbling on a few websites that discuss the topic. These sites reveal how people are always trying to find happiness through distractions, or oftentimes, in their next purchase. Reading more, I also learned how people often refuse to let go of things because they are convinced they may need these 'things' in the future.

Hmm, this was sounding a lot like me. I decided to look more into this minimalism thing. And the more time I spent reading about the subject, the more and more I realized I had some serious distractions in my life. It was like a curtain was lifting.

From there, I was full steam ahead, wanting to live more simply and to be happy with what I already had. I wanted to live in a house that wasn't stuffed with possessions, which actually possessed me.

The obvious: I had too much junk, too many distractions.

And then I started to learn things about myself that weren't so

obvious:
- – I had put too much emotional value in the things that I own
- – Much of what I bought was based out of a need to compete or be like others
- – No one cares what I own or don't own (gulp)

And last, but not least, the clutter that had built up around me was depriving me of things like money, time and energy. But more importantly, this clutter (both physical and mental) was depriving me of something far more precious – inner peace and the chance at having a deeper relationship with God.

In my early thirties I was convinced I should buy a BMW. At the time I was driving a very practical and nice Honda Civic, which was very dependable and gas-efficient. Boring. At least that's what I thought. Plus, people driving luxury cars looked so much more happy … and cool.

So, I spent months looking for a good deal on a BMW. Well, I found that deal. And what I gained was a car that looked nice on the outside, seemingly impressing people (now I know that no one could have cared less) and was in the shop more than it was on the road. I eventually had to sell it at a loss.

Looking back, it's not the money that I lost on that BMW that I regret so much. It's the time I lost spent looking for something I didn't need, to impress people who didn't care. I could have done better things with that time.

Since starting to adopt a minimalist lifestyle, I have also learned that being a minimalist involves more than just taking heaps of stuff to the city dump, selling it or giving it away to charities. It's also about learning to let go of certain non-tangible items too – like friendships that are no longer healthy or positive. And letting go of the past, so you can build a proper future.

Most importantly, I've learned that becoming a minimalist is about removing distractions. These come in the form of thoughts, imaginations, feelings and desires which hold our attention much longer and more strongly than they should.

In the end, the word 'minimalist' is nothing more than striving for a life that is more simple. And in my estimation, a life that is focused less on 'stuff' and more on God.

I have also noticed an extra benefit occurring – my thoughts and desires are being influenced less and less by foolish interests, selfish ambitions and the false standards that the mainstream media and society have unleashed on us in the form of materialism.

So often, we give our attention to what is unnecessary. Is it any wonder why we're constantly distracted in life?

Perhaps it's time to focus on what is truly important.

DEALING WITH LIFE'S DISRUPTIONS

I am a man of routine. I prefer a structured life.

I'm up daily by 5:30 a.m. I read, pray and enjoy more coffee than a person should without having their heart explode.

I go to work. I come home.

I have dinner, read and work in my garden.

I take care of miscellaneous chores and responsibilities around my house. I am in bed by 9:30 p.m.

Lather, rinse, repeat.

Most everyone has a set of habits that serve him or her well. They become easy to stick to over time and we get into the groove of them.

But then something comes along that inevitably ruins everything:

Life.

Everything is going smoothly … you're happy … smiling … content … then suddenly disruptions enter the picture. They show up out of nowhere, and stomp their way through your life. And long after they're gone, it's really hard to get back into your groove.

Disruptions have no concern or respect for your goals, deadlines, schedules and habits.

And not only do they throw a wrench into our normal schedules, they often throw a wrench into our overall spirit. And can even put us into a bit of a bad mood.

And the most important part – they don't have to.

What I've learned to focus on is finding a way to get my peace back when I find that the disruptions are 'getting to me.'

So, if you're a person who tends to become frustrated and stressed out while navigating the major ups, downs and roadblocks of life, what can you do? How does someone conquer these disruptions and get back on track?

Below is a list of six things I've found to be helpful in dealing with disruptions:

1. Expect disruptions and accept them as part of life.

Here we're talking about sudden changes in schedule, problems with the car, computer not working properly, sick children, etc., (or even all these things happening at the same time.)

It's part of life. And when these things happen, it is during these moments that we have a choice. We can 'freak out' or we can work with this new disruption as reasonably and peacefully as we are able to at that moment. It is a process and requires practice. We cannot really *prepare* for it – we only need to be *willing* to do our best.

2. Start to see disruptions as opportunities for growth.

Unwelcome and unplanned interferences in our normal schedules are opportunities to help us grow in patience, understanding and charity.

3. Change your mindset.

If you start to see disruptions as tests that are allowed, or perhaps even sent to you from God, you will start to see disruptions as challenges that need to be dealt with as virtuously as possible, to get back on track. And better yet, to make you a better person.

4. Don't allow the negative.

If you allow disruptions to affect you negatively every time, you'll never improve. In fact, you'll just get worse. Because every time we choose to become upset or angry, versus trying to respond to a situation in a virtuous manner, we become more set in our ways – negative ways.

5. Don't expect too much too soon.

Like anything, it takes time to change our mindset, especially when disruptions mix with our already-established (and rooted) bad behaviors. For instance, when disruptions are coupled with a general lack of patience, this can be nearly crippling for a person. But, it doesn't have to be.

What I'm saying is – don't expect instant results. But keep trying! It takes time, effort and real persistence.

6. When all fails, start again.

Expect failures. But that's certainly no reason to give up.

So, the next time disruptions come on to your scene, and they will, if you feel your pot starting to boil…

Take a deep breath. Pray for help. And then push through it.

Disruptions can disrupt your life. But only if you let them.

THE JOY OF SILENCE

Have you ever noticed how we run from silence and how enthusiastic we are for noise? Noise in our cars – music, radio or audio books; noise at work – music or radio again; noise in our homes – music, radio or television. "… All that noise down in Whoville…"

It seems that we are obsessed with running from silence.

How many people have said, "Well even though I'm not watching it, I like to have my television running in the background for company. I like it for the noise."

Why are we so uneasy about silence?

I think it is because the void it leaves makes us feel idle, dull, barren and perhaps it even seems a bit scary.

So, we fill our lives with noise. And this noise can at times bring with it chaos and clutter.

Several years ago I went on a silent retreat for a week at a Catholic retreat house in Connecticut. And by saying I went there, I mean I was coerced. I had no interest in going but a good friend who had gone kept telling me how great it was.

I remember the drive there. To admit I was freaked out is an understatement. It's not like I'm a raging extrovert (quite the opposite, actually) but the thought of no sounds for an entire week, I found terrifying.

The first day there, I handed in my cell phone. No laptop. I didn't even have any books except the one that we were given to read – "The Imitation of Christ."

During the retreat we prayed in silence, ate in silence, were instructed as we sat in silence and only communicated through hand gestures and written notes.

The first day I wanted to poke my eyes out.

The second day I found myself mentally slowing down, yet still fighting the distractions in my mind.

The third day I felt like the clutter in my mind was starting to dissolve.

The fourth day I never wanted to talk again.

OK, that's dramatic and not true.

But, by the end of that week, I had developed a deep respect and gratitude for silence and the grace that can come from it.

I learned during that week that silence can be beautiful, powerful and healing. I also learned that when you can only talk by writing a note, you only say what's important. I realize now that before the retreat I talked often, but said little.

Silence forces us out of our comfort zones. When everything around us is quiet, we can either grasp for noise to fill that void or we can go inside ourselves. And what do we find there? Often it's things we do not want to find. But that is where it starts. It's only when we discover things about ourselves that need improvement or changing, can we start to let God do His work in us.

So often noise is a means for us to run from ourselves.

Since the retreat, I have learned about several benefits of silence:

Silence can enable us to go within ourselves and find a remedy for stress and anxiety. We can more easily relax if things are quiet. We can remove ourselves from the confusion and chaos of the world and discover many things in our lives for which we can be grateful.

Silence also helps us to focus on what's important. It is only when we are able to find silence that we can be more attuned to the voice of God that is speaking within us, guiding us with how to respond to the situations that come up in our lives.

Silence also teaches us that simplicity and joy are close companions. The more silence a person has in their life the more that they will notice and savor the simple joys of life, without all of the world's many distractions.

Also, silence helps us to realize that a few words well-spoken have far more power than hours of superficial chatter.

It's important to note, that as you create silence by subtracting, that you not fill the empty space with a different type of noise, distraction or clutter.

Let your world go silent if just for a moment. Then try again, but longer. And again.

But instead of letting your mind fill the silence with clutter, try to focus on God within the quiet space that results.

Speak to Him, listen to Him. He will meet you there.

Let God speak back to you. It probably won't be in actual words, but you'll know when He has spoken to you. Thoughts, inspirations, impressions, etc.

You will be surprised how much is actually there in the silence itself if you will just take that first step.

It's there that you will find the joy of silence.

THE MOMENT YOU'RE IN

Have you ever noticed that we rush through our days with so much to do, so much we think we should be doing, and so much we think we're missing out on? But how often do we give the proper time and attention to the moment we're in?

How often when we're at work, are we often trying to quickly get through a task, so we can move on to the next? Or we're simply staring at the clock, anxious to leave for the day?

How often when we're in our homes do we try to quickly complete necessary tasks so we can move on to our hobbies or personal interests?

How often in life do we neglect giving our full focus to the moment? Often, I bet.

The more virtuous way would be to give of ourselves to what we are called to do.

At. That. Moment.

We can always try to find something to be grateful about during the moment of time that we're in. If you're around someone you love, enjoy that. If you're doing something that is providing charity to another, be thankful for that. If you're simply home and secure, be grateful.

But what if you don't like where you are at that moment?

This is when we are provided the perfect opportunity to offer self-surrender and sacrifice for others, and most importantly, to God. A person who lives without peace in their soul is often that way because they do not care to let God manage their lives. Instead, they're always fighting to figure things out on their own.

To do what they want to do.

How they want it done.

When they want it done.

It's here that you are given an opportunity to forget self and find something far greater – the opportunity to let God guide you in what your life should be each day. And no offering can ever please God as the greatest gift of all – your will.

Instead of constantly looking at the clock, wondering how much longer you will be stuck in your current task, now you are given the opportunity to simply give your 'all' to the moment – to the task at hand.

Give yourself to the moment that God has put in front of you at that exact time and place. And by doing it with as much determination and joy as possible, what may have at first seemed displeasing, may even in the end, be rewarding.

Whatever you're doing, whether out of duty or out of charity, most importantly, do it for the love of God.

Remember, it's when we do everything for ourselves that we lose our peace and become selfish. Selfish motives never bring us happiness.

The most virtuous thing we can do is to place our life in God's hands, and let Him direct our daily life as He wills it. This we can do with our patience, understanding, generosity, and unselfishness in our daily activities.

So, the next time you want to quickly get something done, so you can move on to what you want to do – stop for a moment and realize that the moment you're in is the exact moment that God Himself has placed you in. There, in that moment is your opportunity to want to do that task and to do it as well as you possibly can.

And in this moment, you have the opportunity to please God simply by giving your *all* to the task He has given you.

The more perfectly you can give of yourself to the moment you're in, so much the more perfectly you will find peace and a true union with God – and happiness.

And who doesn't want that?

CONSPIRACIES AND CONTROVERSIES

Did you hear that Donald Trump has a body double who helps him out at public appearances that he's not interested in attending?

Did you know that Paul McCartney actually died in 1966, meaning he never duetted with Michael Jackson and never fought with Yoko Ono?

Have you read that the smoke that follows behind airplanes, known as chemtrails, are actually chemicals being released by the government to drop on us from above, with the intention of making us all sick?

Are any of these true?

Maybe. Maybe not.

And what do all of this conspiracies and controversies have in common?

Well, they're all certainly negative and interesting. And horrible, if true.

But more importantly, they often keep us from the bigger picture.

Conspiracies and controversies keep us distracted. And they keep us from giving our focus to where it should be.

And most importantly, they keep us from giving all of our minds and hearts to God.

For years I have walked into discussions regarding conspiracies and controversies. Sometimes they can even become pretty heated. But not one time have I ever heard anyone prove these conspiracies.

And I'm quite convinced that none of these discussions or arguments about conspiracies and controversies brought anyone closer to

God.

Closer to anger? Closer to paranoia? Closer to bitterness?

Perhaps.

But I'm not sure they brought anyone closer to God.

At some time or another, every person dreams of the better person he might have been or may yet become.

If we, like the Apostles, had the privilege of sitting close to Jesus listening to His precious words of wisdom, peace and joy, I doubt we would have heard Our Lord discussing things that *might* be true. Things that *may* be facts.

And if we placed ourselves at His feet for a few minutes (or more!) each day and heard Him tell us how to improve our daily lives, would we not jump at this chance?

With prayer and keeping our thoughts focused on God, we are given the grace to live a better life today. And if we use these graces well, God will grant us even greater ones.

Daily you will grow more like Christ and less like your old self.

But how much can you grow in holiness if you're concentrating so much of your time reading about and discussing shadow governments, false flag operations and chemtrails?

Again, could they be true? Maybe.

But are they facts?

Well, they're definitely possibilities.

But proven facts leave no room for possibilities.

And is it worth it, to overly concern our hearts, our minds, our souls ... on possibilities?

A spiritual man is one who seeks to make the best use of his brief, earthly life. He uses his time well.

He strives to place first things first. And realizes that anything that is a distraction to growing in holiness, is just that, a distraction.

It's definitely a constant struggle to keep our focus, especially in the world we live in – a world that is constantly leading us into speculation. It is a world of *what-ifs*, a world of negative possibilities.

But we must stay focused. Not distracted.

Conspiracies and controversies will always be a part of life.

But don't let these things distract you. A relationship with God is hanging in the balance.

In all concerns and matters, simply do the best that you can do, and pray to God for the rest.

If you suspect that our current president might destroy our country because of an unproven theory you heard … do your best to let it pass.

Instead …

Pray. Pray a great deal.

Focus on growing in holiness. Focus on what matters.

Focus on God.

GOD REPLACEMENTS

I have developed a spiritual routine over the past few years that serves me well. It has helped to keep me focused, driven and on track. But still, sometimes I am reduced by my own willfulness.

Occasionally I find myself reaching for replacements to prayer and spiritual reading.

I call these God replacements.

I mostly blame it on my mood, my schedule and even the season (oh, winter how I dislike you!)

But either way, the result leaves me feeling, at times, somewhat spiritually barren.

For example, my daily prayers, if neglected long enough will gradually be more and more replaced with news, social media or just about anything else I find more interesting.

My everyday practice of reciting the rosary in my car has often been replaced with listening to music.

My evening spiritual reading has at times morphed into spending time with my dogs.

Again – God replacements.

Objectively, none of these things I've listed are bad or destructive. In fact, my dog needs my attention and me.

But I have replaced my Creator with what is created. I need God more than that.

And where do God replacements take us?

In the spiritual life, one must progress. As with everything in life, there are only two directions one can take.

Forward.

Backward.

By avoiding things like prayer and spiritual reading, we avoid progress, and consequentially we're really avoiding God.

We put ourselves at risk of heading in the wrong direction. Perhaps without ever having realized it.

The progress of becoming a more virtuous person really depends on two things: grace and our own determination. And grace is pretty much always at our disposal, if we ask and pray for it ... but it's often our own determination that wavers and changes.

Growing in virtue is not, and cannot be, just about making good intentions. Sure, good intentions are necessary as a start but what's most important is recalling and renewing these good intentions throughout our day. Progress doesn't just happen on its own. We also, with God's help, must act.

Each day we must examine how faithfully we are following our intentions and seek to improve our effort.

Otherwise ... God replacements.

They'll start to show up in our lives. Perhaps even unconsciously. And we put ourselves at risk of becoming someone we do not want to be.

But, when it happens, don't give up! It's never too late to make or renew our good intentions. In fact, we must never lose hope of making spiritual progress. There is still time. And why put off good intentions until tomorrow?

And starting over is easier than you think.

You just need to simply:

1. Examine your life
2. Face what needs to be done
3. Pray to God for His strength and guidance

4.   Start doing it

Make a daily effort and don't turn away at the first sign of difficulty. Try again and again, in spite of repeated failures.

Persevere.

Refuse to quit.

Because if we keep doing nothing …

Then nothing will ever change.

TRUE CHARITY

How often is our intent to be as helpful and charitable as possible to everyone who needs us, so that others may have the peace and help from us that they require?

And how often do we fail at providing this help?

Sometimes we just ignore the call for help altogether. And sometimes we give our help, but perhaps for the wrong reasons.

Often it's in our core attitude towards what we're doing. Are we being charitable merely out of obligation? Out of burden? Or are we being charitable out of love for God?

When our answer is the former and not the latter, the true virtue of charity is lacking. Because true charity causes us to love God above all things for His own sake. It's not about us. It's about Him.

And there is no greater achievement in a person's life than to love God above all other things. And when we are charitable for God sake, not our own, it's only then that charity is in its purest, most virtuous form.

In my past (and sometimes, present) I seek to help others but as soon as things go slightly awry, my act of charity converts into acting out of a burden.

And how often is our 'charity', nothing more than an attempt to gain glory for ourselves? "Look how kind and self-sacrificing I am! I can help everyone and be a wonderful friend! See how incredibly noble I am?"

OK, perhaps I'm exaggerating but this attitude often quietly becomes more and more a part of our general attitude when helping others.

It's during these times that God is no longer involved so much, because much of why we make sacrifices is more about us than God. And when it's about us, and not about God, we start to feel more and more burdened and more incapable of taking care of so many things. We cannot carry the load all by ourselves – but we try to do it just the same.

There is no more room for God's help because we are doing it all by ourselves.

And true charity has no room for our personal likes and dislikes but only for goodness and for doing what is right and for what is needed of us.

Charity is a very holy virtue. One that we must practice, not only during an instance of need but also during every day of our lives. And we must act as unselfishly with other people and situations as possible, for God's sake. Not our own. Because if we're doing it for ourselves, we will always fail. Even if we do everything that is needed from us, we will still fail. Perhaps not in the function of what we're doing to help others but in the reason, the intent, of why we're doing it. Because we're doing it for 'me.' And if we do things only for ourselves, we'll often be left feeling mistreated, annoyed and even resentful.

Sure, we act out of charity for the person we're helping but most importantly we must always act out of charity for God's sake as much as we are able.

And in this charity, we must be patient, kind, thoughtful, helpful and even long-suffering, just as God has been all of these things and more with us.

One of the effects of the virtue of charity, is that it makes us face our own limitations and defects. True charity makes a person humble – because they have to face the truth about themselves and their failures. Even when it's very disagreeable – and many times it will be.

I read once that true charity is the shortest path to God. Because it is the fastest way to the perfection of our souls.

The next time someone asks if you can help him or her in their time of need, say Yes.

But this time, not as a matter of what you feel you can give, but because of what is needed of you – for the help of our friends, family and neighbors. And most importantly, for our love of God.

Simplicity

THE PATH TO A MORE SIMPLE LIFE

I have been intentionally living a more simple life for many years.

There is something very freeing and rewarding about living a life that is simpler. And it's not just about getting rid of possessions. Living a more simple life is beneficial – not only to you, but also to those around you.

For several years now I have been helping to take care of my mother, who is now unable to walk.

It's been a challenge, but with God's help this simplicity has helped give me more peace in trying to manage my responsibilities as a caregiver.

I have been able to remove many unnecessary and unhealthy distractions from my life which, in turn, have added great benefits to my life:

- Less focus on material possessions
- More opportunity to rest
- Creating room for what's truly important
- More peace of mind
- More happiness and less stress
- Freedom from perceived expectations (i.e. everyone else has that or does that)
- A closer relationship with God

As I have slowly moved into a more simple life ... a contented life, I have realized that I have more time and energy (and clear thinking) to devote to higher and deeper things, one of which is helping my mother in her time of need.

And that is what God is calling me to do. And living a more simple life is a direct message from the Gospels.

When you dig deeper, you'll find that living simply is quite similar to the lifestyle that God wants us to live. It's about releasing yourself of all that is hindering you from experiencing a life that God calls you to. It is a call to action to rid ourselves of that which is 'unnecessary' in our lives so that we may gain a strong focus on what really is necessary and what gives our lives true meaning.

God wants us to live more simply, be more modest, live with less, enjoy experiences with family and friends over material things, find peace and contentment and most importantly – focus on following Him.

Jesus told his disciples to sell their possessions, give to the poor and then to follow Him. He warned against greed and the danger of riches and that giving is better than receiving.

That's exactly what having a more simple life is about. Period.

God is calling us to live more outside of our small, self-centered worlds and to serve others more – to give, not only of our money, or of our possessions but also of ourselves.

And over time, and not too long a time, it does get easier.

And it's extremely rewarding.

FINDING CONTENTMENT

I think often in life we seek 'new'. Whether it's a new car, new clothing, a new TV, a new dog, new relationships … you get the point.

And why aren't we more often content with what we already have? Or don't have?

We often tend to confuse happiness and finding contentment with 'things'. We think we can increase our happiness by adding new things.

I've learned more and more over time that contentment is an ability to be happy with what you have or even to subtract from what you have.

It's about finding contentment with who you are. With where you are. With what you have. Even with what you don't have.

Specifically, it's about finding contentment with what God has given you. It is really, at its core, about gratitude. One has contentment, ultimately because one is grateful. That's where peace comes too, by the way.

For many years of my life, I was always searching for more. For the next big thing. For the proverbial greener grass.

Finding contentment and living a life that is rooted in simplicity has helped me tremendously. I still occasionally fight with a desire to want more but I have learned to recognize this as a temptation. And I try to check it at the door quickly, before it takes hold.

Too many times I've witnessed people who have achieved their 'desired level of success' but didn't actually find contentment. Instead they continue to be driven by their persistent want of more and more.

And they remain unhappy with themselves – because when you always want more, it's impossible to be content.

Conversely, I know people that have meager incomes, some that are even very 'poor' and would never be considered by today's standards as 'successful' yet they are happy and have found contentment.

When we're not experiencing contentment, we often make very bad choices. Whether it's bad relationships, bad job selections, bad eating habits or just general bad life choices. Discontent often pushes us to look for things that are not good for us.

We should learn frequently to say to God, "Thank you for not always giving me what I want but for helping me to be grateful for what You have given me."

Because having an ability to look for the good in all the things God gives helps us to actually appreciate and be thankful for what we already have.

Or we can continue the endless cycle of wanting what is 'new' – continue to always want something better than what we already have.

The better option is to find and recognize contentment in your life – contentment with what God has given to us. And hold firm to it.

STOP KEEPING UP WITH THE JONESES

Every day people are faced with making many decisions. Big or small, important or unimportant, this is part of life.

And in life, we have to choose some things in preference to others. But choosing doesn't always involve just 'things.' Choosing also involves philosophies.

Ways of living. Ways of being. Ways of believing.

And often in life, we become trapped into a deceptive way of thinking.

One such deceptive trap many fall into is: That we should have everything. That we *can* have everything. That we *deserve* everything.

It's called 'the more, the better' mentality. The Joneses.

"Life is short, I am only going to live once. So, I want a luxury car, a huge house and a ton of all the latest and greatest gadgetry to put in it."

And when you adopt this mentality, you can't help but start to notice what everyone else around you has. It's natural, when you want the best, you must pay attention to what those around you have. How else can you make sure what you have is better than what they have, unless you are judging what others have?

And so the competition begins, even if you don't fully realize it.

There's just one problem, though …

You. Will. Never. Win.

In fact, every time you try to compete, you'll always lose. Because even if you have the best of something, someone else will come along in about five minutes that will have something better.

It's called, "Keeping up with Joneses." And why should I be interested in keeping up with these Joneses people? I don't even know them!

Often in reality, the Joneses actually aren't who we think they are.

The Joneses live in constant stress and anxiety.

The Joneses have no savings.

The Joneses aren't really happy. Actually, the Joneses are quite miserable.

Trust me, you do not want to be the Joneses.

And the worst part is, the Joneses aren't living for the true needs of their family or for God. They're living for status and admiration, or simply just greed. They're living for themselves.

And when you live for yourself, status, admiration and all these other things that come with excess materialism and consumerism, it's impossible to also live for God.

You cannot have both. It just doesn't work that way.

In my past I was tempted to want the best of everything. But there came a time in my life that I realized that's not how I want to live. There is no peace there.

And once I stopped trying to compete with these annoying Joneses folks and stopped comparing myself and my life to others – the happier I became and the closer to God I became.

When we give all of our time to chasing for material rewards, we leave no room for God. We can try to talk ourselves into thinking we can have both. But we're only deceiving ourselves.

Where your treasure is, there will your heart be also. It's true.

When you choose to desire and live a more simplistic life, one without comparison, it's easier to see God in front of you.

And it's only then, when you see and feel His presence in your life, that you can allow Him to work in you and through you.

The single most important benefit to living a more simple life, one without comparison, is finding God in the space and the freedom that results.

Almost everyone desires peace and a firm, lasting happiness in their life. Living for God, instead of ourselves is greater than any earthly accomplishment, more than any human praise, more than any worldly satisfaction.

Every achievement, success and new possession has its day but quickly passes away. But if we can successfully fight the temptations to consumerism, materialism and excessiveness ... stop comparing ourselves to others ... when we see the 'Joneses,' and we're tempted to think how nice their things are, we'll realize, "They're not real."

But God is real.

And He is happiness. And that's where our focus should be.

HAPPINESS WITH WHO AND WHERE YOU ARE NOW

Spend, spend, spend.

Compare, compare, compare.

More, more, more. Fun, fun, fun.

Have you ever stopped to ask yourself what would life be like if we didn't think that we needed all that? Could we still be happy?

What if instead, we could be happy through simplicity and gratitude? What if we could find happiness and contentment by doing simple things, like going for a walk, reading or spending time in prayer?

And what if by enjoying these simple pleasures and buying and accumulating less, you end up with less debt, less clutter and less stress?

What if we could recognize our wants and desires and then learn to properly deal with them and not be driven by them? What if we could begin to recognize them as addictions, quick fixes and certainly not helpful?

Personally, I've been exploring this myself for the past several years. And while I've improved, I occasionally have some slips and failures. I still find my house has more furniture than is needed. For some strange reason, I still own about 30 t-shirts that I can't seem to part with. And my dogs have enough toys for an entire neighborhood of canines.

But, I've also had many successes with simplicity and contentedness, by following these simple rules:

Say no to impulse buys

Impulse buys are really nothing more than a desire to be happy by doing what other people are doing, a need to 'solve' problems or fill a self-perceived void in your life by acquiring things. I've learned to recognize these impulses and say, "nope, I don't need this." Sometimes after saying "NO" and leaving the store or clicking off the internet page, I'll still be chewing on it in my mind, still wanting the item. But usually within minutes or hours, I've let it go and realized I didn't need it – which I'm sure make my house and wallet both very happy.

Avoid worldliness

Worldly people tend to only think about enjoying their life – following after one pleasure to the next, while giving God and those around them little or no consideration. I know this well, because this was me for many years of my life. I've learned that events, parties and vacations come and go very quickly. And without a relationship with God, the pleasures aren't sustainable in keeping a person happy. By keeping God close in our lives, we can learn to accept and be content with the routine and even the struggles in our lives. And be appreciative of the events, parties and vacations, without feeling like our lives are empty and void without them.

Stop chasing trends

Did you buy that top-of-the-line food processor because you really needed it, or because it was on sale, even though it still cost hundreds of dollars? Did you upgrade to the newest cell phone because you truly needed a larger screen or because television and print ads said you would be happier with it? Learn to be happy and content with what you already have. And trust your instincts.

Recognize that this moment right now is enough to be happy

Often we have a desire to spend, so we can experience what others are experiencing. "John just posted a picture on Facebook of him and

his family at Extreme Adventure Wonderland ... I want to go, too!"
And somehow my life is now less because I'm not racing down a water
slide at 40 miles per hour? And my present (where I am now) isn't
somehow enough? So often in life we aren't satisfied or happy with
what is right in front of us. Develop a practice to pray more and more
to recognize that the current moment, your moment, is already enough
– everything you need is right here, right now.

Enjoy simple things

How often do we look back and reflect only to find that often our
happiest memories came from simple pleasures? I traveled the entire
country of France and thoroughly enjoyed the trip, yet only have a
handful of mostly vague memories. However, I vividly remember the
times that my friend Thorsten and I would sit on my deck, many, many
years ago, talking about life until the late hours with only cheap beers
and uncomfortable lawn chairs to accompany us. Simplicity is often
the key. We can go for walks, spend time in prayer, sit and read a book,
enjoy a steaming hot cup of coffee, play some music, have a conversation with someone (even without cheap beer) or simply do nothing at
all.

To be happy with who and where you are *now* often takes practice.
For some it comes naturally. For others, they must work at it. And most
importantly, recognize when the desire and addictions for 'more' come
to pay you a visit.

These desires will come in the form of advertising, websites, shopping, magazines, seeing what other people are doing and very often
(more than often!) from comparing our lives to others on social media.

The desires will often return but we have a built-in solution within
us. A solution that God has given us, if we ask Him for it.

To help you be happy and content with who and where you are now.
With what you have now. With you.

Overcoming Ourselves

ADVERSITY AND ITS IMMENSE VALUE

C.S. Lewis said, "Hardships often prepare ordinary people for an extraordinary destiny."

And I think he was right.

I have faced many serious obstacles and sufferings in my life. Several of them were some real doozies. And each of them difficult, painful and sometimes scarring. Literally.

Hard work, disappointments, failures, criticism, misinterpretations, opposition, sorrow, death, and bodily suffering are the tests which can show us what we're really made of.

And each of these things, however difficult at the time, can strengthen us and make us into better people. And they can also bring us closer to God.

We all dislike times of adversity. In fact, when they come, we want them out of our lives as quickly as possible. I know I do. But in time, sometimes sooner than later, we are given the grace to comprehend and even appreciate their value.

In fact, it's often the case that our virtues are proved and our faults are revealed during times of adversity.

And it's in these times of adversity we're given choices, which usually come in the form of temptations.

Temptations to run from adversity.

Temptations to follow the easy, comfortable path.

Life cannot and is not meant to be all about enjoyment, fun and leisure. Yes, everyone needs enjoyment in his or her life ... but enjoying ourselves cannot be the sole purpose of what our life is about.

That's called selfishness.

In the end, our greatest achievement on earth is to be united with God in all things. And believe it or not, this closeness to God can often grow tremendously during times of adversity. In life we are used to leaning on others for help – people, institutions, etc. Sometimes when our suffering is so great and all help is gone – it's then that we finally reach out to God.

And that is when we grow.

When life is going well, we can deceive ourselves. We can easily ignore the sufferings and difficulties of people around us – perhaps even those in our own homes.

But not so much when things are going badly. It's then that our faith, hope, charity, humility and patience can be measured only by their testing in real life. When you are going through adversity, you cannot deceive yourself because it's in those moments that you see yourself as you really are – all your strengths and weaknesses come out in full force.

And it's only when we are willing to sacrifice and patiently suffer through adversity, that we are transformed into something more – something better. Because we are, at that time, not thinking of self-fulfillment. We are trying to survive and hopefully trying to trust in God to help us through it.

We also grow more as a person when we can suffer without blaming the situation, blaming others or even blaming God.

So, not only do we suffer patiently but we're also provided with an opportunity to suffer quietly – without complaint.

Our ultimate model for the value of adversity is Jesus' life on earth. From the time of His birth until His last breath on the cross, He patiently endured all kinds of adversity. Quietly, patiently, lovingly, willingly.

Enduring suffering is definitely not easy. It's not supposed to be. But if we can bear it willingly and patiently, we can even find joy, because during times of adversity we are given the chance to exercise more faith, more humility, more patience and more love for others and for God. Instead of favoring ourselves so much.

As I look back on my life and recount the good times, I simply can't neglect the value of adversity, of struggle, of the 'bad' times. Because without the adversity and the struggle – I would never know what is good in my life.

Learn to be grateful for every ache in your body. For every heartbreak. For every disappointment. For every unexpected change of plans.

To feel and to experience these adversities, you will also begin to recognize their immense value, and to clearly understand they were presented as opportunities from God.

To become a better person. To love Him more.

And isn't that why we're here?

ANGER MANAGEMENT

In general, most people tend to prefer peace to conflict. We definitely prefer calm to tension. Yet, anger still shows up occasionally to rear its ugly little head.

And being angry, when it comes down to it, is because of one thing: selfishness.

Nearly every time we get angry, it's because something (or occasionally, the entire universe!) is not going our way.

Anybody can get along with those who are quiet and mild-tempered. And associating with people you naturally like, or with people who tend to agree with you, is no great accomplishment.

But the true virtue of overcoming anger is proven by getting along with people and situations that are difficult and even contrary to our own way of seeing things.

Personally, I tend to become angry with people that I 'view' as being prideful, selfish, rude and thoughtless.

In the past, when I detected this in a person, not only did I want nothing to do with them (at least in the moment it was happening) but I would also make sure they knew I was annoyed by it.

Was that virtuous of me? Umm, I highly doubt it. How about judgmental, too?

The better position is to live not only at peace with ourselves but to also be at peace with those around us, regardless of their actions.

"How dare this person treat me this way!"

"This person needs an attitude adjustment, and I'm just the guy to do it!"

Or, instead...

"This person must be going through a really hard time right now, I should see if I can help him."

"This person needs my prayers."

"Perhaps this person just needs me to be a better example."

Our best way to avoid selfish anger is to be more compassionate, versus retreating to our inner spoiled little brat that didn't get his or her way about something.

And. It's. Not. Easy. Let me tell you.

Personally, my inner spoiled little brat has bright red hair, fangs and eats far too much chocolate.

Think about it, how often are we exactly like this brat, except we're grown-ups and are supposed to know better?

When we're busy, someone interrupts us and ... bam! Angry time! Why? Because we wanted to continue our work uninterrupted but some inconsiderate troll has ruined that perfect world (you're obviously seeing how wrong this is, yes?).

So, how do we turn our reaction of anger into a response of peace and calm? First, by bearing patiently what we cannot remedy. If someone needs to interrupt you, I'm sure (for the most part), they truly need your help with something. And a person who knows how to suffer this patiently, will be rewarded with peace.

And if we do it for God's sake, the reward is all the greater – as well as the peace.

When troubles come to us, we should do our best to not let these 'troubles' disturb us. If in the end you're not able to find immediate compassion for the person or situation (the universe!), look to God, Who, with prayer, will help you to find the peace that you need.

Again, anger often appears when things go against our wishes. What if instead of anger or spite (internal or external) we live by a good example letting our patience rule the situation or the day?

I used to work with a woman who was always happy. She was continually smiling and positive. At first this woman annoyed me because I thought she was fake. But then I quickly realized just how genuine she was.

And the most interesting part? I learned with time that this super happy, always positive woman had suffered many painful trials and obstacles in her life. But she never seemed the least bit resentful or angry. Her faith in God is strong, and her positive personality reflects her love for God.

Each time we counter, with patience and humility, those people and situations that annoy us or make us angry, we diminish the selfishness and pride that used to rule in us. They have less and less hold on us.

Don't get me wrong, there are rare occasions for 'righteous anger' but admit to yourself, how often do those occasions really happen?

Most of the time we become angry because we lack understanding, sympathy, patience or even a willingness to suffer any more than we must – or even at all.

How would Our Lord react in these same situations? He is our ultimate model. Letting go of anger isn't easy. But as we become more aware of the people and situations that incite anger from us, we are given opportunities – valuable opportunities – life-changing opportunities. And you know what 'they' say … never let an opportunity go to waste.

SAYING GOODBYE TO BAD MOODS

Have you ever been asked "are you in a bad mood?"

And sometimes the question varies a bit.

"Why don't you smile more?" or "Are you upset about something?"

"Did you receive word that a zombie apocalypse is coming?"

OK, perhaps not the last one, but personally I have gotten these types of questions more times than I can count.

And I'm always left wondering why do people often perceive me as being a grump? I mean, don't get me wrong, I definitely have days that I'm not in the best of moods. We all have our share of bad days but generally I think I'm a pretty happy fellow.

But it's my firm belief that when bad moods do come it's often because of various bad habits that we have developed over time, which enable the bad mood to show up – and stay for an extended visit.

Conversely, when we form good, healthy habits, they can become a path to good experiences, outcomes and even good moods.

Below is a list of some bad habits that can often end up derailing our peace and put us into bad moods.

1. <u>People-pleasing</u>

When a person spends too much time trying to please others because he wants to be liked, versus just being who God created him to be, it can end up making a person very unhappy. If you simply focus on pleasing God and doing what is right, peace and happiness will follow. Also, there will always be someone who does not like your decisions. So what?

2.   <u>Being too hard on yourself</u>

"I can't do that," "I'm going to mess that up" and my personal favorite: "I'm not even going to try." And these statements are usually said to ourselves, not out loud. And how do we know we can't do it? Shouldn't we at least try and find out? Learn to give yourself a break.

3.   <u>Being pessimistic</u>

This person is a perpetual half empty glass of water, and their first thoughts or reactions to situations tend towards the negative. It takes a lot of time, prayer and effort to break this one. Especially the older you are. But, it can be done, with God's help!

4.   <u>Perceiving a future outcome that doesn't exist</u>

And not only does it not exist, but when the future becomes the present, the picture that was painted is rarely (if ever) the reality that actually happens. Learn to live in the present. That's where happiness exists.

5.   <u>Unable to take criticism well</u>

If you're unhappy with something I've done, am doing, or didn't do – I'm the absolute last person you should tell. Does this relate to you, perhaps? By God's grace, we should learn to evaluate criticisms in order to use them constructively so we can improve and not just become offended. Let's face it, you're not perfect. Nor is anyone else.

6.   <u>Being a worrywart</u>

Most of what we worry about, we have no control over. Why should I worry about a storm knocking out my electricity or coming down with a cold before I leave for vacation? This is how it feels to be a worrywart: stressing over inconsequential things and building false scenarios in your head. If we can just take a moment to step back, think about all the things in our past that didn't turn out the way we worried they would, we'd realize it's not worth the worry. But actually, is worry ever worth it? Umm, no.

Basically my point in all of this is: happiness is the result of good decisions but we need to first adopt some good habits, and rid of ourselves of the bad ones. It's the only way to turn a bad mood into a good mood.

Avoiding a bad mood takes practice and time and a lot of prayer and help from God … especially if your negative habits have been lifelong. Work diligently to rid yourself of the bad habits that cause you to become negative. And don't forget to pray and ask God for a lot of help. Together it will vastly improve your outlook, your peace and your happiness.

And you can say goodbye to your inner grump.

GAINING PATIENCE

Let's face it, we're living in a growing culture of impatience, which conditions us to crave more and more instant gratification.

For me, I can become irritated waiting for an internet page to load. If I'm working on a project, I want to have it finished … today. Actually, yesterday.

And I'm described by my friends and family as being laid back!

Recently, I decided to stop at a fast-food restaurant. The drive-thru line was long, wrapped all the way around the building. My first reaction was to say, "forget it" … but I stayed. As I sat in my car, I started to get more and more frustrated. I fumbled with my iPod for music to keep me entertained. I checked my phone to see if anyone had messaged me. But I couldn't focus, I was becoming more and more frustrated with the long line.

Finally after about five minutes I was second in line to the order menu. Life would go on, things were going to be OK.

But they weren't OK. The man in front of me about to order his food spoke into the microphone and said, "I need a minute to look over the menu." I couldn't believe this; he had already had five full minutes to think about what he wanted.

Then, when he finally began to place his order, he started asking questions about the menu items.

I sat there looking in amazement. I quickly looked in my rear view mirror. Surely the person behind me was as annoyed as I was.

After what seemed like an eternity (probably less than a minute), his order was complete and he drove forward. But it was too late! I was annoyed and my peace was lost.

I placed my order and then ate my food while still feeling annoyed.

Taking a look back at that experience, I've realized some facts. First, between the long line and the person in front of me, I felt as if that completely ruined my peace that afternoon. I even felt as if it ruined the enjoyment of my sandwich.

But, it didn't.

The line and the person in front of me didn't ruin anything.

I did.

That guy ordered his food smiling, drove away smiling, and he enjoyed his food, probably smiling. He had no idea I was even upset. He didn't hear me murmuring behind him. He was at peace. He did nothing wrong. He had every right to take his time reviewing the menu. And he had every right to ask questions about the menu. The only person that ruined my peace – was me. I had the ability to keep my own peace and patience that afternoon – and I failed.

When I look around me, I see similar reactions from other people, whether it's anger with drivers, checkout lines, people telling long stories, etc. We live in a 'get to the point' society.

People seem more and more impatient that ever. Perhaps it's due to our society's demand for instant results? Saying this though, I realize, not everyone reacts the same in these situations.

I am always impressed when I witness other people practicing patience. And what impresses me most is their consistency. A truly patient person does not change their demeanor given the situation. They're patient with everyone from their superiors to their equals. They're patient whether they're dealing with others that are well-meaning or rude.

Recently I took my mother to a doctor's appointment. When I registered her in at the receptionist desk, I was informed that the doctor was running behind. My mother wouldn't be seen until about an hour after her scheduled appointment.

And it wasn't just my mother's appointment. All of the patients' appointments were running behind schedule. As I sat in the waiting room, I noticed that everyone around me seemed annoyed. I heard people whispering things to each other like, "this office needs to get their act together," and, "this is ridiculous, making people wait this long."

As I continued to observe, I noticed a woman sitting with her young daughter. The mother and daughter were smiling and laughing. I could hear them talking about the details of the daughter's day at school. They had to wait like the rest of us, but they were OK. Why?

When the woman and her daughter were finally called as the next people to be seen, the nurse who came to get them apologized for the delay. The mother smiled and said, "No worries, we were enjoying our time waiting."

What was different about them? Why were they so patient? I didn't ask but I think I have some good guesses.

I believe that one aspect of patience is the disregard of one's own convenience or inconvenience. That mother and daughter didn't register the experience as anything personal against them. They just made the most of the situation. They realized that in grand the scheme of things, the long wait really wasn't a big deal.

Their example made an impression on me. And it left me wondering, how does one do it? How does one become more patient?

I've since learned that two things can really help a person to be more patient: Prayer and common sense.

When I am praying to God for help in this, I start off by saying, "God, please help me with my patience!" – just like that. That clearly. That quickly. I let Him know that I need help and I need it right now. I will also pray that God helps me to be more humble. When you think about it, if people were more humble, they wouldn't be so impatient. Impatience is often a feeling of, "I don't deserve this."

We should also ask God to remind us of our own faults, limitations, and defects, so that we can focus on improving ourselves first when we are tempted to be impatient, especially when my impatience is the result of judging the actions of those around us.

Lastly, we need to remind ourselves to be patient with *having patience* and that everything is in God's time, not our own. And sometimes it takes a long time with many trials and errors along the way.

Next come the common-sense elements of the equation.

1. Sparks

When you become aware that you are losing your patience, pay close attention to the things that spark this. Certain sparks occur more frequently than others – and these are the things to work on first. Using my example from earlier, waiting in line at a restaurant, if you're about to encounter a long line, or a similar type situation, you can mentally prepare yourself thus resulting in more peace.

2. Breathing Deeply

As impatience creeps in, take a deep breath … and breathe out slowly. Another. And another. It works.

3. Perspective

In the here-and-now things can often feel frustrating and annoying, but if you take a step back (mentally or literally) you'll probably realize, things aren't as bad as you originally thought them to be. I can't tell you how many times I have been frustrated or even angry, but when reflecting on it later, find the reality of the situation to be quite humorous. Hours and sometimes even minutes can completely change our perspective. By learning to recognize early that your perspective might be different later, maybe you have a chance 'now' at not becoming so impatient or even angry.

5. Charity

Often (actually, almost always) impatience stems from selfishness. Frankly, thinking too much about our own wants and desires and not enough about the people around us. When we start to think more of other people and less about ourselves, it's only then that we can truly start to become patient.

Patience is something you will always have to work on, especially if you have an impatient personality (like me). And in the process, there are times that you will fail. But you will never make progress unless you start doing something about it now. And the peace you will start to experience in your life will soon make you realize that it's definitely been worth the effort.

"Have patience with all things, but, first of all with yourself"
— Saint Francis de Sales

CHANGING OUR JUDGMENTAL CHARACTER

In almost every show or movie there is a character that is completely annoying.

You know exactly whom I'm talking about.

They're mean, constantly complaining, gossiping, wimpy and judgmental. Basically, they're annoying and you just don't like them.

I've always wondered if I were a character in a movie, how would I be perceived?

I would like to think that I would find my character nice, helpful and maybe even somewhat humorous.

But those are on my good days. How about my bad days?

If I were to see myself in a movie, as an observer, I might not always like my character. In fact, I might even dislike him.

Think about this, too. When there is a character in a movie that is annoying, judgmental or even wicked … and in time they start to change for the better, what naturally happens to us as the viewer?

We want them to be better.

We begin to like them.

We even start to root for them.

Take Ebenezer Scrooge for instance. A terrible, horrible, judgmental person. He is truly an awful person, and I doubt anyone goes into that story liking him.

But near the end of the story, when he 'wakes up' and becomes a better person, you start to like old Scrooge. You just can't help it.

Personally, I have had many moments in my life that I'm not proud of. And sometimes within hours, or heck, even minutes, I'll think to myself, "Wow, I would totally hate my character in a movie right now." Especially when I'm being judgmental.

Because when I become judgmental, I become the character in the movie who I'd like to give a good punch in the head.

So, how does one conquer their temptations to judge others? Well, initially, by keeping them just as temptations. When the thoughts to judge others come into your mind, try your best to get rid of them or simply ignore them. Eventually they will go away, but only if you do not give in to them.

In the end we really need to mind our own business and not set ourselves up as judge, jury and executioner to those around us.

We should also remind ourselves throughout the day that when we are tempted to be judgmental towards another person that there is also a good deal that we do not even know about that person.

When we fall into judging others, it's very rare that we will ever judge justly. Only God can do that – only God knows the heart. We never will.

Instead, it would be much wiser to think the best of other people and leave all judgment to God.

An interesting thought, too – we have our own faults to contend with! It's better to look at oneself with a more critical eye, rather than those around us. In fact, unless you've tapped into a magic spring of perfection, you can keep fairly busy just correcting your own faults.

As for the faults of others, the best you can do is to be a good example, offer a bit of advice if you are asked and pray for others, versus criticizing and gossiping about them.

By not judging others, you will have more peace in your own soul.

One of the worst faults of human nature is that of condemning others. That is why Jesus taught His doctrine of charity. As we judge others, so will God judge us. If we condemn others, so too we run the risk of being condemned. A true follower of Christ is more ready to think well of others than to think evil.

In your life, try to no longer be the movie character that is judgmental towards others, picking out people's faults and failings. The movie character that everyone wants to punch.

Instead, be the movie character that recognizes and works to diminish his own faults and failings.

That's a character you might even like – a lot.

YOU CAN'T CHANGE OTHERS, ONLY YOURSELF

People are the worst. They don't do the things we want them to do. They don't respond the way we want them to respond.

They're rude. They're inconsiderate. They're selfish. And this often leaves us annoyed, angry, frustrated, disillusioned, and constantly wanting to change others.

And I'm officially sick of it.

I've decided that everyone else on this planet is wrong, and they're against me. And they all must die!

OK, I'm being a bit dramatic. But isn't this how we often tend to feel? Just minus the cruel deaths.

Sometimes we tend to blame (externally or internally) the people around us for our own general malaise.

"Work has been too stressful!"

"This person was totally inconsiderate of my feelings!"

"He was just totally rude to me!"

"Humanity as a whole is shaking its fist at me with unlimited offenses!"

Sorry, too dramatic again. But when it comes down to it, we can tend to blame other people for our own frustrations. And the result: we want and desire to change others.

This is a mindset that many of us share. And the reality is, we will always be frustrated if we stick to this mindset. In fact, this way of thinking about others will only leave us constantly angry, upset, offended and greatly unfulfilled.

But, there is another way of seeing this problem. However, this way of seeing things may be hard to accept though.

Brace yourself!

In reality, those around you, annoying you, are almost never the problem.

It's you.

Hear me out. We should never excuse other people's rudeness or even their meanness. But, many people in our lives will be rude, arrogant and inconsiderate. It's just a reality that we can't control.

But it's our *response* that we *can* control – with prayer, virtue, practice and determination.

For every person that is unpleasant to us, we are given an opportunity to respond in a calm, peaceful and virtuous manner.

We can counter their coldness with compassion. We can smile when they are grumpy. Many times if we respond this way often enough, a more virtuous response on our part can help to transform the other person to follow our lead. I have seen it happen.

The oddest part is that the people that are frustrating us with their behavior, are usually quite clueless to the effect it causes in us. Most often, people are far too consumed with their own life and issues to even take notice. So, if you're expecting them to change – don't hold your breath.

Instead, pray for them.

Only God can change the heart of another person. Not you.

If you continue to have expectations of how other people should act or behave – you've already lost.

Throw your expectations out. Stop trying to change others. Instead, try to merely accept that the person in front of you, the person that is totally annoying you at this very moment, is a flawed human being. Much like yourself.

Try also to examine your own notions of how other people should act. And realize that if you are holding onto this impression, it is in conflict with reality.

As long as you embrace fantasies that aren't in line with reality, you will always be frustrated. Or you can keep trying to make the actual reality match a false reality that is based on your expectations.

Umm, yeah, good luck with that.

Instead, stop blaming others for not acting and being the people you want them to be. Show them compassion and patience instead. You may learn something valuable about yourself.

Again, we should never excuse rudeness, inconsiderate actions, selfishness or even flat-out meanness. But what I'm suggesting is that we should first start taking action – with ourselves.

Let go of your frustration. Pray for the people that are upsetting you. And stop trying to change others.

People can only change themselves. But not without some help. Specifically, they'll need your help. And this help will come in the form of your prayers, your good example and your patience.

And remember, there is always one person that you can change – you! Do you prefer to be constantly upset, mad or even incensed? Or would you rather let go of all the expectations you put upon other people and react in a calm, pleasant manner – being a good example to others?

Today you are given an opportunity to try your best … to smile and act with compassion and patience.

And the other person … you know, the rude, difficult one … may be taking notice.

Impediments to the Spiritual Life

OVERCOMING FEAR – THE ONLY WAY OUT IS THROUGH

Recently I spent time with three of my family members from England. They came to the U.S. specifically to visit my mother, who is their aunt.

During the visit the stories that were shared brought true joy. My mother hadn't been so happy in years. Sharing stories. Hearing stories.

And the constant smile on her face was a wonderful reward.

However, when my British family members first announced they were coming for a visit, I felt nervous.

How would the visit work, given that my mother is confined to a wheelchair?

How would I be able to properly entertain them?

Would their visit be too much for me, as I am introverted and prefer 'visiting' in small doses?

Would they regret their trip?

As it turns out, these fears were just that – fears.

My fears. Not theirs. Not my mother's … Mine.

And sometimes fear has a way of crippling us and stops us from doing what is right and often necessary.

I can't tell you how glad I am that after explaining to my family that it might be best they don't come … that they came anyway.

I am immensely grateful for their determination and for ignoring my fears.

And I thank God for helping me to push past my fears.

In life sometimes fear is necessary. For instance, it can help us to stop doing something that is dangerous or something that is just plain stupid. But in reality, most fears are unnecessary, unfounded and simply hold us back.

And if experiencing fear is a natural human occurrence, then it's up to us, with the help of God, to decipher when fear is stopping us from growing closer to Him and experiencing the happiness He wants to give us.

And then with the help of God we push through it.

Many of the fears we experience are simply unfounded. They can often come in the form of, "I am not good enough; I am not strong enough."

When we let God help us to overcome these fears of failure and rejection, we almost always succeed. But what does 'succeed' mean then? It means you will have grown in your trust in God, in your courage and strength. It does not mean that you won't have some scars and bruises along the way.

So, how do you do it? Face your fears and push through them?

There is no definitive guideline to overcoming fear but the following works for me:

The first step is to acknowledge your fear. When you realize you're afraid of something, regardless of what it is, think about it, pray about it. Most of us simply try to ignore our fears, so we can move about our lives without the interruption. But fears cannot just be 'wished away'. They only become worse.

Secondly, let yourself experience the fear. Realize you're not the only one who has this fear, regardless of how small, large or rare the fear seems to be.

Personally, I have a fear of being around more than four or five people at one time. Most people would think that's a silly kind of fear but for me it's very real. So, whatever your fear is, you're definitely not alone.

Third, pray to God for help to overcome your fear. This is the only way it will happen. The most important part of overcoming fear is that we need to rely on God and not ourselves. Obviously we are not strong enough to do it alone, or we wouldn't be afraid in the first place, right?

Fourth, realize where the fear is. Most likely it's in the future. In fact, fear is almost always an apprehension of an unpredictable future and a negative spin on what 'could' happen.

You're trying to predict a future that you can't possibly predict. Unless you've suddenly developed the skills of prophesy?

Learn to live in the present versus dwelling on what 'might' happen. Stop allowing yourself to even consider the future. The future will be there soon enough. Live in the moment. It's much harder to fear the present.

Fifth, begin your attempt of overcoming fear slowly but surely. Don't run from fear – push through it. Be grateful for every success, and brush off every failure.

What are you waiting for?

Start facing your fear today. I have a feeling that you'll be glad you did.

COMBATING STRESS

I don't need to describe stress. We've all become stressed at times, and we all know when it's happening.

But what is important to learn is how to rid ourselves of stress.

When stress enters my life, interesting side-effects start to happen to me.

For me, my body and my entire countenance start to become clenched. I become irritable about everything. I feel as if I'm in the midst of a battle, and I become grouchy and defensive.

I call this my 'ugly' stage.

And when I reach this ugly stage, I work hard to get out of it quickly and with the least amount of damage to myself and to others as possible.

And this is only achievable because of two things: trust in God and gratitude.

Have you ever noticed that when stress enters your life, you feel like you've lost control of the situation? Why? How about because things aren't going they way you want them to go?

And when we lose control, this causes fear, anxiety and stress.

First we must let go of this need for control and instead trust in God for help and for the answers. By doing this we will come to realize that what we perceive in the situation as chaos and uncertainty, in the grand scheme of things, is not as bad as we had made it out to be in our own head.

When life throws us an inevitable curve ball and we feel like the obstacles are too much to handle, what do we do? Where do we turn?

There are choices. We can become frustrated, annoyed, or even angry. We can try to avoid the obstacles and stress by retreating into bad habits for consolation. But guess what – they will still be there!

Or …

You can take a step that sounds difficult but is surprisingly simple. You can put your trust in God.

Think back to every stressful and bad situation that you've had throughout your life. I'm sure there have been some real doozies. But then think, did it work out in the end? Maybe not all of them as you had hoped, but I bet that most of them really were not the horrors that you made them out to be.

So, instead of freaking out, why not ask God to help you with your problems? Ask Him for the answers that you can't think of yourself. Learn to put your complete trust in God. He will not only get you through but you will truly grow to rely on Him, versus relying on yourself. Who's going to fix this problem better anyway – you, or God?

Once you start to put your trust in God, you can usually get yourself out of the 'moment' of feeling stress and anxiety; and start to realize things aren't that bad. You can relax and let your muscles stop clenching. You can breathe easily again. You can even smile. Not a forced one but a real smile. Why? Because the burden of this problem – this cross – is no longer on you, who cannot carry it alone, but it is now also with God, who wants to carry it with you.

Have you ever had a friend that seems to be able to maintain a relatively positive attitude regardless of what stress they're dealing with? They seem to have an ability to focus on the positive, even when they're in the midst of hard times. People like this tend to focus on challenging situations as being opportunities, but most of all, they are grateful for what they have, even in the face of negative, stressful times.

In the past when I felt stressed-out, I would often feel trapped in my present obstacles and the fears and stress that came with them. I often had to challenge myself to be grateful. But when I was able to do so, I was able to realize that I do have so much to be grateful for and that God has given me so much.

He has also given you so much.

Gratitude helps us to see our situation in a way that can lessen stress and can often give us the ability to think clearly of new solutions to our current problems.

Think to yourself of all the things in your life that you have. All that God has blessed you with.

And so what if suddenly your car breaks down, or you're given an assignment at work that feels too challenging, or you're feeling sick … or worse? Is the world, or even just *your* world suddenly coming to an end? Do you need to allow stress into your life because of this current situation that will soon be in the past?

No.

Because God will always give you all that you need at every moment. Even when life is challenging.

Know this.

Believe this.

And then you can live this.

LISTENING MORE, AND TALKING LESS

There really is a skill to listening.

Not talking … not whistling … not singing.

Listening.

It may sound silly but many people honestly do not know what true listening really is. We know *how* to listen, I'm just not sure that we always really *do* listen.

Things like distractions or on-the-fly created responses often get in the way of people really listening to what another person is saying.

For me personally, to listen well doesn't come easy. In fact, listening is hard work!

I've learned through many years of experience that if you truly want to listen to another person, you need to absolutely lose your desire to want the other person to think like you do.

Wait. That's worth repeating.

You need to absolutely lose your desire to want the other person to think like you do.

I can't deny that it's human nature that we prefer to associate with those who agree with our own ideas. That's how friendships usually start. But not always. Sometimes being too opinionated and outspoken can often destroy friendships.

And, you'll never be able to truly hear another person … everything they're saying … unless you are truly focused on and attentive to what they are saying.

And when we're listening, we need to let the other person finish what they're saying and wait before interjecting with our own thoughts and opinions.

A good listener will always learn more than a person who talks too much.

I used to make this mistake a lot. Talking and not listening.

A while back, a friend of mine was telling me about an upcoming trip to France that she was planning. As she started to tell me about some of the sites she was going to visit, I completely interrupted her, telling her about when I went to France. I told her about my favorite restaurant, my favorite museum. I even told her about the cow in the south of France that nearly ran me off the road.

After I finished talking, she smiled, excused herself … and walked away.

And I was left standing there, by myself, feeling like a complete idiot. And an annoying idiot at that.

It was obvious that when the conversation started she was clearly excited about her trip, attempting to tell me about the places that she was going to visit and the things that she was planning to do. But she never got the chance, because I completely railroaded the conversation. My main role in that conversation was supposed to be listening.

And I failed.

It is not always necessary to correct or even add to conversations. I think we sometimes feel compelled to always have something to add to a conversation. But why? Isn't it nice when someone listens to everything you have to say, versus having someone constantly interrupt you?

In fact, those who know how to hold their tongues have more interior peace. For there is a certain uneasiness, or perhaps even an insecurity, that comes with always wanting to interject with our own thoughts and opinions. Not to mention, it's quite self-centered.

It's also best never to think too highly of our own thoughts and opinions. Even though we may treat them as such, opinions are not facts.

When you think about it, it really does take a certain amount of humility and real charity to listen well and not always voice our own thoughts and opinions. It is humble because it's our nature to want to be heard and it is charitable to let the other person be heard – without interruption.

Pray to God for help that He will show you how to be more considerate and attentive to other people when they're speaking. Pray that He will help you to listen more and talk less.

And practice.

A lot.

STOP COMPLAINING

It took me far too many years to come to a realization. I was a complainer.

In fact, I was always trying to be more positive and not complain, but it never seemed to last.

And through a lot of prayer, it finally dawned on me. To stop complaining, to stop being negative – when things aren't going the way I want them to go – was never going to work, unless I worked on myself from the inside out.

I used to always think that I just need to stop complaining outwardly, but yet on the inside, I often remained annoyed and frustrated. And I learned that to truly have a better outlook on the things happening around us (i.e. not complain about them) we must learn how to recognize what is going on *inside* of us.

Before speaking, it's essential to be aware of our thoughts and feelings. It's also essential that when we realize that we're feeling negative on the inside about a person or situation, we must then start at that moment to pray to God for help.

Think to yourself, " Why I am feeling so negative?" When you really dig down, it usually comes down to one simple reason.

"It's not fair. Things are not happening as I want them to. And I just don't like it."

Once you realize that you feel slighted, or unjustly treated, you must also realize that to continue thinking about it in this way will only serve to make you miserable and this will not be beneficial in any way – to you or anyone.

Now is a time to 'problem-solve.' Problem solving is the opposite of complaining, and it is so much more productive!

You will also need to shape a new way of thinking – one that has God as its focus. A more virtuous way of seeing things.

To truly stop complaining, and to be successful, it must go beyond, "if you have nothing good to say then don't say anything at all."

If you're still thinking about it, the negativity is still there in your mind, just no one can hear it.

It. Is. Still. There.

You. Must. Kill. It.

As with any disease, it needs to go, because if it's still there, then you are merely suppressing it.

Instead, pray and be a keen observer to your internal world. It will take diligence. It will take patience. It will take hope.

Note though, when you decide that you want to start taking on this interior cleaning project, situations will invariably come up and you will start to experience these negative feelings and temptations to complain. Something or someone will start to get on your nerves. But before you start to put a scowl on your face, or look over to your friend or co-worker to express your negative thoughts …

Don't.

Don't move.

Don't speak.

Just don't.

Instead, first realize your impression may be completely off base – even if you think your viewpoint, feelings and reasons are so solid that they could stand up in a court of law.

How many times do we over-exaggerate our viewpoint on a situation? How many times have we wrongly passed judgment on another person?

Let it go. It is probably not as bad as it you perceive it to be.

Instead, when negative thoughts enter your mind and you feel the need to complain … do your best to dismiss them. Don't let yourself expound on them. Don't become attached to them.

You have to kill them as soon as they come up or else they will take hold.

If you are able to keep a distance from negative thoughts, you'll soon notice how quickly judgments and complaining happen in your mind. You'll start to see just how routine it has become for you.

And only you, with the help of God, can break that cycle.

When we allow our mind to give in to this way of thinking, we can start to imagine many things that make us even more negative. Things that distort our reality.

And if you've been thinking and reacting this way for many years, changing won't be easy but with prayer, diligence and God's help, you will change it. But you have to *want* it.

And when you're able to actually give up complaining, you will fully realize just how much it was a part of your life.

But better yet, once you're able to give up complaining …

You'll experience far less stress.

And you'll be more content.

You'll be happier.

LIVING IN THE PRESENT FOR A HAPPIER LIFE

Growing old is inevitable.

Sure we can dress young, act young and even color our hair to make us think we're young.

But, at a certain point, you will be confronted with a jarring realization: you are closer to the grave than the cradle.

I once watched a movie about a group of former famous musicians. In the movie, these musicians who were widely-popular and respected during their peak performance years (1960s – 1980s) were now much older, with their glory days tucked away in the distant past.

Now older, each had gone on to spend their remaining days at a retirement home designed especially for musicians. This way they could continue to spend their remaining years doing what they love best, playing music and being around other people who share their love for music.

But what struck me as the most interesting thing about the movie, were the differences in the three main characters.

The first character denied his age, always trying to look and act much younger. He tried to project a persona that was carefree and happy but on the inside he was constantly worried and borderline despondent about the uncertainty of his future.

The second character clung to her past. As a result, she was often dark, sad and bitter. She constantly daydreamed and obsessed about her past triumphs and glories, refusing to accept or be content with her current reality.

The third character accepted his age and was generally happy and pleasant. He had his good and bad days and always managed to stay upbeat, humorous and positive. He was living in the present.

The first character was tormented by a future he couldn't predict.

The second character was defined by a past that no longer existed.

The third character lived pleasantly, day to day, experiencing joy and working through difficulties as they happened.

Watching these characters made me realize that as we all get older, there are three different paths we each can take.

Living in the Future

This path includes constant stress and worry of what may come. The person who mentally lives in the future is often very stressed, uptight and even paranoid.

Will I have enough money to retire properly?

Will there be anyone to take care of me?

Will I get cancer?

Will I…? Will this…? Will anyone…?

This person wastes his present life to stress about the future.

Living in the Past

This path includes thinking and reliving (in our minds) all of our past happy times and victories, coupled with a crippling sadness that these days are over, never to return. This path can also include self-pity, with much time spent wallowing in past regrets.

And unfortunately, a person who goes down this path spends a lot of time wishing for their past to return, either to relive it or to do it over differently – a concept that no one has ever been successful to make happen. Nor ever will.

Living in the Present

This path is taken by people that realize the past is exactly that – the past. They may have fond memories of the past but their mind doesn't dwell there.

They also realize too that the future is not predictable, so beyond making some common sense preparations, they do not give the future too much consideration.

And most importantly, this person realizes that life on earth is finite and tries to live each day to the best of their ability for God. They're living in the present.

Each of these three paths contains a full spectrum of emotions and challenges but living in the present is by far the easiest and most rewarding to navigate.

We never 'try' to live in the past or 'try' to live in the future. We just do it. It really doesn't take any effort – we just go there according to our natural inclinations or weaknesses in our personality.

To live in the present, we actually must 'try.' We are not always inclined to do it. We often must force ourselves. It takes work. Darkness can keep us in the past or in the future, and avoid the present. The present is where God is now.

The present contains far less problems.

The present contains far less sadness and stress.

And the present contains far more happiness.

The best thing we can do with our past is to occasionally reflect back on good memories, or even past mistakes that make us better. Looking at it from a strictly common-sense perspective, the past is not happening anymore, except in our minds … if we let it. So don't stay there. The past is a place of reference, not a place of residence.

The best thing we can do with our future is to let God take care of that for us. How often does the dreadful future we predict for ourselves actually happen? My guess is, rarely. God will give us everything we need if we completely trust in Him. We must trust Him more than ourselves and He will actually have a chance to help us!

So try, as best you can, to always live in the present. God is there and wants to be involved in your life – right now. Not yesterday, not tomorrow.

Right here, right now. He's here for you.

THE DANGERS OF HUMAN RESPECT

We humans have a sad tendency to take good things and distort them. Consider human respect, for example. God's good plan for us has always been for us to honor, value and respect one another. In our fallen world, though, where every virtue gets distorted into a corresponding vice, too often we twist honoring others into pursuing their respect, and putting their opinions ahead of our reverence for God and our duties toward Him.

Frequently this pursuit shows up in the form of fear: fear of not fitting in, or of being criticized for thinking or acting differently from other people, especially when it comes to practicing our faith. It's a matter of fearing man more than God; being more concerned with what other people think of us, than what God thinks and expects of us. This unholy fear often causes us to make bad decisions to avoid upsetting others, or being looked down upon by them.

Ultimately — we care too much about what others might think of us.

This shows up in all kinds of ways in our day-to-day lives. One way is in our silence when we hear others promoting or praising something we know is wrong, but fear of rejection or ridicule leads us to say nothing. We hear Our Lord's Holy Name being blasphemed, or we hear others refer to good as evil and evil as good, and we know we should speak up against it because it offends Our Lord — but we say nothing.

Or perhaps someone is in our care, whether it be a child or an employee, and we know we should correct them because they are doing something wrong, but we say nothing out of fear of losing their respect or good favor.

It's only natural that we want other people to like us. But at what cost?

Our goal should be to always live life in God's presence and according to His Will, not according to what might cause others to speak well of us.

Easier said than done, right? But remember, all things are possible with God.

To live like this takes the courage to do what we know is right, and do it for God. It means being brave enough to stand out from the crowd and not to simply take the safe route, the popular route, the easy route.

Many people are afraid of being different, or worried that they may appear intolerant or backwards in their thinking. They may simply be afraid of standing up for what is right — alone.

The question we should keep asking ourselves though is, am I following God? Am I following what has been passed down from the Holy Scriptures and the teachings of the Church?

If we simply follow the popular opinion, we will always be fitting in with the crowd, at best. At worst, we'll be thinking, believing and acting in a way that's offensive to Our Lord.

People tend to judge each other by their own likes or dislikes, or by their own set of fixed ideas — and this judging is opinion-related. But it is impossible to make everyone happy. And you'll end up exhausted and probably pleasing no one. Our Lord will only ever judge our actions by how much we have demonstrated our love for Him, by following all that He asks.

We must instead trust God enough to be willing to do what we know is right, what God expects of us, even at the risk of being embarrassed or judged in a negative light.

The thoughts and words from those around us can neither add to nor subtract from our true worth. You are not a better person when you're being praised or less of a person because someone faults your way of thinking and believing. Your only goodness, along with the goodness of everyone around you, can only come from God.

So give up on chasing after human respect. Never avoid doing a good deed or performing what is right, through fear of being rejected or hurt by another person. Stand firm in your faith and in what you know is true.

It's better to walk in the right direction — even alone, than to go with a whole crowd that's headed in the wrong direction.

Because the one who walks with God never walks alone.

Seasons of Change

LENT – A TIME FOR SPIRITUAL SPRING CLEANING

Who has a stronger conflict than he who strives to overcome himself?
– Thomas à Kempis

I have always been amazed at just how spiritually beneficial the season of Lent is.

How wonderful it is. How valuable it is.

And yet I'm always glad when it's over.

I think it's often hard to transition from the spirit of Christmas, to a spirit of penance.

But the reality is, that if you do practice Lent in the spirit it is intended to be practiced, it's certainly not easy. But, of course, I don't think it's supposed to be.

Lent is a time to meditate on the Passion of Our Lord – to think about how much He has given for us – everything. It is a time for us to look into ourselves and think what we can offer back to Him. Especially the attempt to overcome things inside us that are not very nice – a time to put into practice new virtues.

Through Lent, we reflect on the life of Jesus, and through Him we take a deeper look into our own lives.

It's a time to make an honest assessment of where we are on our path (and our struggle) for holiness.

We are each given opportunities to give up various things for Lent, which could include certain foods, coffee, alcohol, movies, news, social media, restaurants, time out with friends … the list is endless.

And each year we can add things, as well. Like spiritual reading, being nice to people that we don't normally want to be nice to, smiling more, being more patient, listening more, being more charitable...i.e., things that do not come naturally to us.

And with time, giving up certain things and adding certain penances during Lent, our understanding of the sacrifice that Jesus made for us grows deeper and deeper, resulting in a more profound gratitude to Our Lord and greater changes within ourselves.

When you think about it, Lent is kind of like a spring-cleaning but for the soul.

And we all know how much better you feel once you've done a little spring-cleaning.

ADVENT - A PREPARATION FOR CHRISTMAS

As each year draws to a close, and Christmas fast-approaches, we tend to focus on what is obvious – putting up our decorations, trimming our tree, shopping for friends and family and eating every type of dessert known to man.

And before you know it, time has escaped us.

Suddenly it's Christmas Eve night and all the wonders that come with it – reflecting on Bethlehem, the birth of Jesus, the angels singing, the shepherds in the field, the wise men beginning their decent from the east, all reaching the pinnacle of, "Silent Night, Holy Night."

But wait! Are we even prepared for Christmas? Prepared for all of the beauty and wonder of Christmas? Truly prepared?

Before the coming of Our Lord, is the season of Advent. A time of preparation.

The world tells us that Christmas is about filling our homes with bright lights and greenery, attending office parties, singing carols, listening to "Handel's Messiah" or the latest pop star's new Christmas album. The world encourages us to shop, shop, shop!

I love Christmas just as much as anyone (maybe more). But should we not also be more intentional (and joyful) when practicing and experiencing the season of Advent? The coming of Our Lord!

And what should we be doing to prepare for the coming of Our Lord? The obvious things are:

– Meditate on Our Lord's impending birth

– Give to those in need

– Feed the hungry

– Clothe the homeless

– Be kind to others

But perhaps it is not possible for you to go out and help the 'homeless.' That's fine – OK, then how about helping those in your own home?

What ways can we prepare our hearts for the coming of Baby Jesus – in our own homes? How about patience – toward those nearest you? Be more willing to listen, less eager to criticize. Give of your time and your person and not necessarily of your money.

We can also practice more patience with those outside of our homes – especially in stores or driving on the road (Christmas shopping traffic!). We can be more giving and patient toward those in the workplace. Maybe we can be less prideful and more humble.

How about being more temperate with our sweet tooth (or teeth, for that matter)?

Advent challenges us to understand the Christmas season in the contexts of the coming of Christ. Advent also offers us a powerful alternative to the commercialization of Christmas. A reason to exclaim, "Merry Christmas!" instead of a bland and politically-correct, "Happy Holidays."

I'm sure you've heard it before – Christmas is a season for giving.

Then make it so. Give to those in need.

I'm sure you've heard that Christmas is a time for feasting.

Then make it so. Help to feed those around you who can't afford to do so.

I'm sure you've heard that Christmas is a season of joy, hope and peace.

Then make it so. Grow in these virtues by putting them into practice with friends, family, neighbors and strangers – and most importantly, with the whole reason there is Christmas, for God.

And the next time someone asks you, "Are you ready for Christmas?" you can honestly say, "I'm not but I'm trying to be with the help of the season of Advent."

A Better Way
of Thinking

HUMILITY IS TRUTH

I'm sure you've heard it before. A humble person is a happy person. It's also very true. Humility is an important virtue to possess.

A person with true humility experiences joy in their life by recognizing and acting on what God has called them to do, regardless of what the world might think about it.

So many people today are quite miserable, constantly comparing themselves to others that they consider to be smarter and more successful. But the humble person has the ability to be content with who they are. And with that comes freedom and happiness.

But as we all know, it's not exactly easy to put into practice.

Having confidence in the abilities that God gives to us is important. It helps us to perform well at work and in our relationships. But overconfidence in ourselves – well, that can result in an over-inflated ego.

We must never forget that all of our abilities and talents are gifts from God. This realization alone is an important and essential key to humility.

Also, many people think that humility is simply an interior sense of weakness or inadequacy or perhaps even a lack of properly appreciating oneself. But in reality, humility is far from this. It's an honest assessment and admission of facts, versus feelings – and then acting accordingly.

People that are truly humble live their lives free from posturing, never trying to appear "better" than they really are. They simply evaluate each instance for what it really is, by the honest facts, which helps them to see things more clearly, and to act more objectively.

When you think about it, there is just so much pretense in the world today. Everyone is trying to outdo other people, often trying to appear better than they really are.

But are we working harder to be a better person? To live a more virtuous life that is pleasing to God?

On a personal level, being honest with myself, I must admit that I have many faults and failings. And I can point them out faster than anyone else can.

So, when someone does point them out to me, do I let these opportunities cause my pride to rise up and say, "How dare you??!!" or do I consider and realize that perhaps they have a valid point that I need to consider and accept, so that I may improve?

God is pleased when a person lives a good, honest, truthful life – a life that does not expect a return of praise and thanks for everything he does.

True humility brings peace.

Pride brings chaos and unrest.

Remember – God is humble. Jesus is humble.

So, the next time someone wounds your pride …

Take it as an opportunity to assess the honest facts and to act accordingly.

That is true humility.

WORRY CHANGES NOTHING.
PRAYER CHANGES EVERYTHING.

Growing up I was a bit of a 'worrywart'. I worried about everything. Every. Single. Thing.

Whether it was school, my family, my looks, my popularity (or lack thereof), I was a walking ball of nervousness. I was the kid you passed in the hall and thought, "What the heck is wrong with him?"

As I got older my worrywart ways continued but for slightly different reasons. Popularity and my appearance weren't as much of a concern (thank you braces and contacts), but things like college, employment, relationships and money (or lack thereof) took over as the new big things to worry, obsess and overly-focus on.

It wasn't until my thirties that things changed for me. I started to relax. I became content with what I had or didn't have. And the pressure to compete seemed naturally to fade away.

But the biggest difference was and always will be – allowing God into my life. And trusting in Him.

Before you start to think, "Oh listen to Alan, all high and mighty. Mr. No Worries"… rest assured – I will always have the worrywart gene pulsating within me, cycling through my blood stream. It's something I will always have to constantly fight against. And I do.

Consider this:

What did you worry about a month ago? Can't remember? Right, me either. But whatever it was, it occupied our thoughts and our time. And it certainly wasn't positive.

What worries you right now? Is there anything you need to do about it and reasonably can do about it? If there is, then do it.

If you're always worried about arriving late for work, then simply do what you can to get there on time, or early.

Set your alarm clock in the morning. Give yourself enough time to get ready. Get in the car. Go to work. Done.

But if you're worried about the possibility of your child getting sick and delaying you ... or, will there be road construction that makes you late ... or, will Hurricane Zelda flood the roads, or ...

Get the point? Let it go.

Do what you can easily do. Then, occupy your mental and emotional energy with something more productive. More positive.

People who worry all the time always want to be in control. And that's understandable. Who the heck doesn't want to be in control? But there is only one problem with that.

You can't control everything. No one can. And in the end, trying to control everything around us is bad for us – and for those around us.

But nevertheless, the worrier will always try to gain control. They have to do something! And when it doesn't work, they'll either concoct new ideas to gain control or obsess over things. Even to the point of despair.

So what's the alternative if you can't control things? If something is beyond our control, beyond us changing it for the better – pray. Because God is in control, if you let Him be.

Try your best not to worry about anything; instead, pray about everything.

Tell God what you need, and thank Him for all He has done for you.

For instance, if you have an upcoming meeting at work that you're stressed about, what are your alternatives?

Properly prepare for it? Check!

Stress that it will go the way you hope?

Obsess about the possibility of the meeting going wrong?

Be a disaster?!

Being humiliated?!!

Fired from your job?!!!!!

Just reading this, can you feel the tension? The stress?

And what good does it do you?

Instead, do something that is incredibly simple: Do what is reasonable to prepare, and let God take care of the rest.

If you do this (with lots of practice), you will experience God's peace, which is more wonderful than the human mind can comprehend. His peace will guard your heart and your mind.

Everyone falls into the trap of thinking that they can manage their daily life without any guidance and assistance from God. That includes "yours truly." I often go about my business without consulting Him. I trust myself alone.

And when this happens, worry and stress always return. But with prayer, trust and help from God, no person, no thing, no event, will ever have control over us. Because God has control of these things.

Not us. Him.

In all things, simply do the best that you can do, and pray to God for the rest. Never worry about the things you can't control. Or the worry will end up controlling you.

Worry changes nothing. Prayer changes everything.

DAILY GRATITUDE

How often do our days feel like fast-paced, stress-filled messes? Whether it's from a hard day at work, caring for a sick child or suffering from the worst head or stomach ache imaginable.

And when we have a day like this, it's hard to have gratitude for anything.

Imagine after a long, hard day, pulling into your driveway. You turn your car off, pause, and take a deep breath. It's as if the day has stolen your breath from you.

And after taking this deep breath … you thank God. Simply because He has given you another day.

And even though in the midst of the stress and suffering, you realize that tomorrow is a new day, and with God's help, you can try again.

Because tomorrow is another day to be as virtuous as you can be. Another day to grow closer to Him.

You have so much to be grateful for.

This really is the only response that life truly deserves: one of gratitude.

This day, wherever you are, however your day went, take a moment to think about all that you have to be grateful for. Regardless of how hard the prior day, week or even the year has been.

I bet if you think hard enough, you'll find it. Your Gratitude.

But don't stop there.

It's time to move forward and to give back to God. Do something, anything, to show your gratitude for the graces you've been given.

And, if you've been stressed, or perhaps not as virtuous as you know you can be, then simply ask God for forgiveness and the strength to be better on this new day, or this new hour, or this new minute.

Let it go. The very next moment is new. Begin again!

When you stop to really think about it, a new day is something within itself to be amazed and grateful for. Every day is new. Every day is an opportunity to start over.

Gratitude keeps our hearts humble, it helps us to see everything as a gift from God and helps us to focus our lives on others – versus always thinking of ourselves.

Letting gratitude extend to all things, even when things are less than pleasant and difficult is not always easy but it's very important. And the odd thing is, being happy shouldn't be our cause for gratitude.

Ding, ding, ding.

Instead, being grateful can help us to be happy. If we try.

Today you can make an extra effort to be kind to someone. To create something others will derive benefit from. To be a source of strength for others. A source of hope for others.

Life was never meant to be perfect or filled with daily excitement. Work is often challenging and even sometimes boring. People will often let you down.

But if we learn to stop just briefly during our day to ponder the true wonder of life, the true wonder of God's gifts to each and everyone one of us – it's at that moment that we can fully realize what a wonder and a gift life truly is!

We just have to take the time to recognize it.

To see it. To appreciate it. To be grateful for it.

To thank God for it.

One of the things that continually astounds me is just how much I have to be grateful for. Another thing that continually astounds me is *how often I forget* just how much I have to be grateful for.

If we began to count the blessings that we truly owe to God, we would never finish counting, because each added moment of life is another gift.

The best gratitude we can offer Him is to use His gifts properly. And instead of an occasional, "Thank You," we ought to shout it with our every breath.

Gratitude changes lives. Let it change yours.

ACCEPTING AGE

Age fascinates me. It always has. And this fascination has progressed and been molded into different thoughts, realizations and fears as I have gotten older.

And who wants to be old? I know, I know, I've heard the arguments for age progression. Statements like, "I have earned every wrinkle on my face," or, "the pains in my body are my battle scars," or better yet, "I'm so much wiser now than when I was in my 20s." And you know what? As true as those statements may be, at the end of the day, getting older is sometimes hard.

Well, at least it's hard when looking at it from a superficial and worldly viewpoint.

In my late 30s I grew my hair out long. I looked ridiculous, but it was my way of not accepting (and rebelling against) the fact I was closing in on 40. When I see pictures of my hair that long now, I must admit, I have a good laugh. But at the time, I thought I was so much cooler than other people my age.

Since having turned the tide into my 40s, I have found the only way to age and to truly be OK with age is to simply accept it and not try to fight it. Wanting to be young forever, quite simply, is a very dangerous game to play. Perceptions and priorities become out of alignment. People become trapped in and long for their past. So, I won't be growing my hair long again.

And you know, beyond the vanity of one's appearance, and the pains and perceptions of age, there is something much deeper to consider.

As my clock ticks on, my thoughts have turned towards my faith and God and not about bucket lists or other superficial things I think I need to do before I die. Sure, some fun things are great to do, but these things shouldn't be our goal.

Part of getting older is realizing that life is incredibly short and that God asks many things of us. Things like attempting to be more humble and charitable and to remove vain and needless distractions so we can focus on a closer relationship with Him. And a constant attempt (and often a struggle) to become less of a worldly person and more of a spiritual person.

And often as we get older, what used to be important or first in priority to us is simply no longer important and certainly not first. Things like job titles, status symbols, friends who aren't really our friends, and possessions, which often end up possessing us.

So, whether you're 20, 40, 60 or 80, it's never too late to think and pray about what is truly important. And when you are old (by the grace of God), and you're looking back on your life, you won't be reflecting on your past career titles, expensive sport cars or other vain glories. You'll most likely remember the times spent with friends, family and the things that reminded you to be grateful for all of God's blessings.

We all have lots of things to accomplish before our clock on this earth stops ticking. Not the things that we wanted 20 or even 10 years ago, but the things that God has shown us that we need now.

THE HEALING POWER OF FORGIVENESS

The world has become an angry place. In some cases, a dangerous place. In many situations a place of harm and damage and injury, more than many of us can remember. I speak not only of what we hear in the news. Everyone experiences anger and harm and injury and loss sometimes. The Bible says to forgive (Matt. 6:14-15; Col. 3:12-15). Does that really make sense, though?

Yes.

Holding resentment towards someone else is like drinking poison and then waiting for the other person to die.

It took me many years to realize this. Far too many years.

Thankfully, after finding my faith, I also found a couple of other things.

Compassion. Trust. And most importantly – forgiveness.

I think there is a human condition where many people assume that if we forgive others for the wrongs they do to us (or those close to us) that we are, in a sense, releasing them from any responsibility when perhaps they should be punished. The offender gets to go on merrily through their life while we are still haunted by their actions. So, if we forgive someone, perhaps we are only condoning the wrong that they did!

Not so.

Forgiveness is a necessity for us, not vengeance. God is the true judge, not us.

And God doesn't just ask us to forgive others, he commands us to forgive others. It's not an option. And God is certainly not foolish, callous or capable of ever being wrong. He can't be. He's God. And when He commands something from us, it's because it's for the best. For us and for everyone involved.

God knows that by allowing ourselves the freedom to forgive and forget (yes, we must forget, too), we not only find peace, but we are saying in essence, God is the only judge in all things.

In fact, we may not have committed the same crime that we're upset about. But we've committed other crimes, haven't we?

In each of our lives, we've all been hurt at times by the actions and words of another. And this often leaves us fuming mad, very hurt or even tempted to feel vengeful.

It's OK to be upset. In fact, it's good and often necessary to call someone out on something they've done wrong. It's OK to tell the other person that what they did was hurtful.

But we still must forgive. It is necessary.

By not forgiving, we're essentially stating, "Yes, I've committed my own crimes, perhaps crimes that are different, or maybe even the same – (maybe even worse!), but we're not focusing on me right now, we're focusing on you. And you are so very wrong and awful and disgusting and completely sub-human for what you have done."

And in reality, our own sins and wrongdoings should displease us far more than any one else's. Let's face facts; it's our own soul that we should be most concerned with. And by condemning, judging and not forgiving others for their misdeeds … well, that is in no way helpful to our own soul. We are consuming the poison of blame and condemnation ourselves.

What then is the outcome of an inability to forgive? Someone who can become bitter, mean, resentful, untrusting, suspicious and eventually – spiritually dead inside. Very often, the effects of refusing to forgive take a physical toll as well.

Conversely, if we identify the wrong that was done against us and concretely and sincerely forgive that person – many times over and over if need be – not only is it pleasing to God, it's helpful to ourselves. If we don't practice forgiveness, we might just be the ones who pay most dearly. By offering forgiveness, we also bring upon ourselves blessings from God – peace, hope, gratitude and even joy. Forgiveness leads us to physical, emotional and spiritual well-being.

Forgiveness is good for our soul.

Forgiveness is necessary for our soul.

Forgiveness is imperative for our salvation.

O Lord, forgive us our trespasses, as we forgive those who trespass against us.

If we are contrite and repentant, God will always forgive us our trespasses. He asks us also to forgive those that trespass against us – both inside and out. We must also let go of all interior thoughts and feelings of any resentment or a desire for revenge.

In reality, the wounds from acts that have hurt or offended us may always remain a part of our life, but forgiveness allows us to free ourselves of their grip on us and helps us to focus on other, more important things – such as compassion and prayer for the very people that have hurt us.

Remember, forgiveness doesn't mean that we deny the other person's responsibility for hurting us, and it doesn't minimize or justify the wrong. Forgiving someone doesn't equate to excusing the act. But forgiveness brings us peace, so that we may go on with our lives and please God.

When I had my terrible car accident, the person who hit my car ran a red light, driving well over 60 miles per hour. It was completely his fault and I was left with many injuries that took months to heal.

When I lay in the hospital that first night, I was angry and was feeling very sorry for myself. "Why did this happen to me? I did nothing wrong. I didn't deserve this. He did this to me," I thought to myself.

And as those feelings started to take hold, I was given the grace to recognize what was happening. I decided that I wasn't going to drink the poison that comes with resentment. And that night I forgave the person who put me in that hospital bed. To my surprise, I even started praying for him. And I have honestly never had a negative feeling about that accident since, or towards the person that caused it.

I've made mistakes in my life. I have done and said things that have affected others negatively. I have hurt others. I still make mistakes today. Who am I to not forgive another person for something they have done wrong to me? I know I certainly hope to be forgiven when I make a mistake, whether it is a minor infraction or a big one.

Making forgiveness part of our daily lives is essential for spiritual and personal growth. It may be difficult at first but by God's grace, it becomes easier. I can tell you from experience that you'll be glad you did.

HAPPINESS IN FIVE SIMPLE STEPS

Have you ever wondered if there is some kind of magical way to find happiness?

Well, I'm sorry to tell you – it doesn't exist. But there are 5 simple steps that can help a person to obtain happiness.

Let me be as up-front as I can.

I personally don't believe you can be happy all the time.

There, said it.

But … I have learned that you can be happy much of the time.

But it often takes some work.

It's important to understand that being happy isn't dependent on how your day is going or how others are treating you.

Being happy does not depend on your environment.

Being happy depends on you.

You are in control of your mood.

You are in control of your demeanor.

You can control your own happiness.

It's your own choice. With a little help of course.

Maintaining a strong relationship with God and following these five simple steps (with lots of practice) can help you find happiness:

1. Prayer

The more we pray, the happier we become. When we pray, we become less anxious, and we are filled with greater peace of mind and heart. Because we give our problems, concerns, fears and decisions over to God.

The more we pray, the more we understand ourselves because we come to know God more. And we begin to see God in our day-to-day life – acting in our life. And our relationship with Him becomes meaningful. It becomes real.

This doesn't mean to imply that things will always go our way because 'everything going our way' is impossible and unrealistic. But if we try to see God's will in our lives we can be more capable of gratitude for the good times and trusting in His strength during the bad.

And it's important to note when we stop praying, that's when things will begin to go wrong for us.

We were created for prayer. If the very purpose of human life is to know and love God for all eternity, then the purpose of our lives is prayer – communicating with Him and getting to know Him better each day.

There will definitely be times in our lives that are filled with difficulties, heartbreak and even deep sadness.

If we turn to God in these times of sorrow and difficulty, if we rely on Him as our strength, if we do not give up but press forward through the difficulty – on the other side we will be stronger, we will be better. We will be happier.

2. Never Envy Another Person

Being happy for others may not come naturally for everyone. Especially when we have a competitive spirit. But when you find you're able to feel happiness simply because of the blessings in others' lives, you gain a fresh perspective on life.

Also, being envious wastes a lot of time and energy. When you sense that you are becoming jealous of someone, you should let go of it immediately, which will leave you feeling unburdened. You will feel free.

Always remember, the success of others isn't personal. It wasn't done to spite you. It costs nothing to remove your own desires from the equation and feel relief and happiness for another person. When God has blessed another human being, we have no right than to feel anything other than happiness. Not just for the other person but for ourselves. Because we have much to be grateful for as well.

3.   Living in the Present

I have mentioned this earlier but it's worth repeating. Happiness will never be found in our past. Whether it is longing for days gone by or regretting what can no longer be changed.

Equally, happiness cannot exist when we're overly concerned with our future.

The best thing we can do with our past is to occasionally reflect back on good memories, to be grateful for them, or even past mistakes – to be grateful for them, too! – because hopefully we have worked with God to become better from them.

Looking at it from a strictly common-sense perspective, the past is not happening anymore, except in our minds … if we let it. So don't stay there.

It's also important for us to realize that the future is unpredictable, and worrying about it is a waste of time. The best thing we can do with our future is to let God take care of that for us. God will give us everything we need if we completely trust Him. We must trust Him more than ourselves and He will actually have a chance to help us!

Focus on *right now*, and you'll always be able to handle what comes.

4.   Live Simply

Living simply is the intentional reduction of clutter, whether it's stuff, obligations, expectations or even people.

God wants us to live more simply, be more modest, live with less, enjoy experiences with family and friends over material things, find contentment and most importantly – focus on following Him. It's here, in this simplicity, that we can find happiness. Otherwise, we're always looking for the proverbial greener grass.

5. Give More, Expect Less

When we give of ourselves and expect little in return, happiness follows. Whether it's giving a smile, an hour of your time or a simple 'thank you', the sincerity of the action can mean a great deal to the receiver and to you, as well.

It's impossible to be happy when we are only thinking of ourselves.

I repeat: It's impossible to be happy when we are only thinking of ourselves.

By this, I'm not suggesting you to volunteer every weekend or donate 20% of your income (unless you want to). But by giving of yourself, it takes the focus off 'self'. Charity is one of our most precious virtues and is extremely pleasing to God.

Everybody wants to be happy. It's true.

Instead of attempting to find happiness in transitory, fleeting things, try simply living a life that is more positive and meaningful, with God at its core.

By doing this, you won't need to constantly seek or buy your way to happiness. Happiness will find you.

The truth is, you can skip the pursuit of happiness altogether and just be happy.

The Importance of Our Soul

PEACE OF SOUL

Surely we can do, for one day, that which seems impossible for a lifetime.

In other words, the process of taking one day at a time. It's certainly not easy, but it is often necessary.

It's a sad fact, but it seems that high stress and countless anxieties, whether they come from work or from our home lives ... well, it seems to often be the modern way of life.

Our sense of peace and calm seems to be something we have to strive for. And often the sense of peace and calm we hope for simply doesn't happen. At least not on its own.

Peace and calm always need to start from the inside.

Sure, we can find peace and quiet while sitting on a beach, taking a hike in the woods or relaxing with a cup of coffee. But it's how we deal with our day-to-day life that helps us to find interior peace. Even in difficult situations.

In life we bear many crosses and when we bear them unwillingly, it's then that we find them to be greater burdens than they already are. And yet we still have to bear them. A person who runs from their cross is only running toward another cross, perhaps even a heavier one.

In life we should try our hardest not to avoid our problems or find ways to run from them.

Instead we should pray to God for Him to strengthen us and help us to stop avoiding them.

We can never truly know what our tomorrow will be but on this day, if we find it to be hard, we just have to get through it. With God's help and support, of course.

And the more and more we rely on God to help us through life's difficulties, the more and more we find ourselves growing even closer to Him. Because we learn that we need to turn to Him more to get through life's bumpy roads.

Personally when I try to rely only on myself to solve my daily problems and remedy my troubles, I only end up frustrated, angry … and complaining a lot. I fail.

But when we learn to embrace our cross, our burdens and our sufferings, we find God standing with us in the midst of it, waiting to help us. And it's then we realize – I don't have to carry this weight on my shoulders alone.

And with God's help, through all of life's many difficulties, we are given a gift that is very important:

Our self-control.

Our patience.

Our peace.

And we also find that we will naturally begin to rebel less and less against God's Will.

The, "I want to figure it out my way!" syndrome.

It's definitely a growing process, learning to fight the desire to avoid the trials that come our way.

But with God's help, we will better deal with our hectic schedule.

We will hold our tongue when things and people annoy us – at least a bit longer than our natural self has in the past.

And the more we grow in our love and trust in God, the less we will run from difficult things.

All of this will help us to better achieve a greater sense of peace within our soul.

Your soul.

At the end of the day, it usually comes down to selfishness, "I want this … I deserve this."

For a person who begins to or simply wants to desire nothing more or less than God's Will, peace will come.

Resentment against the circumstances in your life will only rob you of peace of soul.

By learning to live with what you cannot control or eliminate, God will help you to rise above such things. Only God can help you to have peace in your soul.

Give Him the chance to share your life … with Him.

Surely we can do, for one day, that which seems impossible for a lifetime.

(With God's help of course).

That should be our motto. And as it turns out, it's a pretty good one.

Are you ready to experience more peace in your soul?

FINDING SOMETHING THAT IS LOST

New challenges that pop up in our life, regardless of the level of difficulty, bring the realization that the other aspects of our lives must go on. In most cases, we still have a job and responsibilities at home that require our time and attention. But with God's help, one can to adapt to changes.

"A new normal," as I've always called it. You know what I mean. When things change – and it's not temporary.

It takes time, patience, prayer, faith … and, well … perseverance.

And often when things in our life go awry, unfortunately bad habits and faults often return to rear their ugly little heads.

And the virtues we have worked so hard to obtain, suddenly become more of a challenge to maintain. It's during life's challenges that we find ourselves being impatient, judgmental, anxious, selfish, etc. … the list goes on and on.

And it's during these times that we spend our time trying to find (and retrieve) something that is lost.

It's also during these times that we can fall into self-doubt or even despair. When this has happened to me, I notice a little devil on my shoulder whispering to me, "Alan you're a hypocrite, who are you to write a blog on virtue? Just last week you cut off a slow driver and gave him a dirty look. And let's not forget how you yelled at your own mother."

Ouch.

And it's at these moments that we realize we have lost some things that are very valuable – the ability to comprehend that we are all a work in progress – the ability to understand that with every failure we are given an opportunity to start anew – the ability to realize that a true path to virtue takes a daily effort.

Some people in life refuse to even consider an effort to improve their lives. Some actually make a half-hearted attempt but turn away at the first sign of difficulty.

Please don't.

I have learned that we must try again and again, in spite of our repeated failures. And by refusing to quit, our failures will occur less and less.

In life, with the help of God's grace, we can only do our best to fulfill our resolutions. We cannot judge our progress by our feelings or by visible signs or by receiving praise from others.

All we can do is to purify our intentions, concentrate on the virtues we wish to improve upon and to strive to eliminate our own self-love in the process.

Becoming a better version of you will never be achieved in a day. Perhaps not even in a month or a year. But one thing is for sure – it will never be achieved at all if you never start working. It's only with this determination, this continued sense of perseverance, that we can find something that is lost.

Our peace. Our gratitude.

Even our willingness to suffer, in order to help ourselves or others in need … or simply to do what is right. No matter how hard things get or how tempted you are to give up.

Remember, one step at a time. And you're never alone.

With God's help and guidance.

PEACE THROUGH DAILY PRAYER AND FAITH

Life is busy. But of course, you already know that.

You also know that when things turn stressful, your day can quickly turn from pleasant and peaceful, to, well, anything but.

And to help relieve this stress, you can try many different things to bring back your sense of peace – alone-time, a glass of wine, a good book, a walk outdoors, etc.

But would it not be better, instead of relieving your stress, to prevent the stress and tension from happening to begin with?

And that's exactly where prayer comes in.

When we can learn to pray before things go awry, even when things are currently peaceful, we have a better chance of dealing with the stress and tension when it comes.

Because when we learn to pray to God that He will help us to be in union with Him, in whatever happens this day, good or bad, we have a much better chance of ending our day with a smile, versus a seemingly much-needed glass of wine.

Just imagine having a peaceful, calm day when previously that concept seemed unattainable.

Imagine car rides to and from, never feeling the need to rush anywhere. Simply allowing people to drive the way they want to drive and just flowing along with the traffic, no matter how fast or congested it is.

Imagine caring for a sick child, while you're also trying to do ten other things and just doing the best that you can do, knowing that some things simply will not get done.

In life, we often tend to pray for special intentions, friends and family that are sick or in hard times, or for world situations.

But how often do we pray for our day-to-day life? How often do we pray for help and guidance with our normal tasks, normal duties – things that come with every day? And by neglecting this, we limit God's potential in our lives.

We should learn to make a concerted effort to include God in all of our daily activities.

In every decision. In every action. In everything we do.

When we are stressed out or feeling anxious, it's mostly because we want to be somewhere at a certain time or want something to happen the way we want it to happen. We desire other people to be (or drive or talk or react) the way we want them to, and we become stressed when they simply don't comply. And many (if not most) of these stresses we feel are entirely self-created.

We tend to create our own anxiety. And we think we have the solutions to solve our own day-to-day problems.

It's only when we turn our problems and our daily tasks and duties over to God that we are able to gain peace. Because when we allow God into our daily lives, our interior peace is no longer disturbed by daily events that are beyond our control.

When we pray and commend our day to God, asking for His help, it's then that we become less attached to our own desires and no longer complain when things are not going the way we wanted.

It's when we pray and commend our day to God, asking for His help, that it feels so much more easy and natural to be kind and compassionate to others – even those whose actions and personalities are not in compliance with our desires for them.

It's when we pray and commend our day to God, asking for His help, that we better deal with the stresses of our lives, instead of complaining about them or running away from them.

It's when we pray and commend our day to God, asking for His help, that we can learn to give proper attention to every person and every duty in our lives, without giving them too much or too little.

Your desires will gradually become less focused on yourself and more focused on God and His desire for you. He will take care of all the details. If you let Him.

With a commitment to daily prayer, and faith in God that He will help us through our daily lives, we can attain peace and calm in the midst of the raging flow around us that is called 'life.'

Prayer, and the faith that God will answer our prayers – these two things are essential.

When you have succeeded in giving yourself to God, without any reservation, then God will give Himself to you so completely that you'll neither need nor desire your old ways of managing the stresses of this life.

Prayer. Faith.

THE POWER OF PERSEVERANCE

A common struggle in the lives of many people is a tendency to bail on things.

When someone raises their voice at us, we're ready to walk away.

When life becomes what we feel we didn't sign up for, we start seeing greener grass somewhere else.

Whenever we're in a funk, we start to consider other options.

When we're in a rut, we seek our escape.

Basically, sometimes, we have a tendency to want to do away with what no longer feels natural or easy to us.

I used to struggle with this myself. And actually, I didn't even realize I was like this until I made a connection.

I had just left a job because I no longer liked being there. In fact, I had really grown to dislike it – a lot.

A few months after having left the position, that is when I made the connection – I have walked away from every job I've ever had.

I simply decided that I had had enough, and left. Just like that.

I wasn't a jerk about it. I gave two weeks notice, and in two cases, six weeks notice. But regardless, I decided it was time to bail.

In fact, I had always wondered why other people stayed with things for so long.

And after making this connection, I started to see it as a lack of perseverance on my part. And then I started to see it in other areas of my life, too. Relationships. Exercise. Diets … the list goes on and on.

But wait. After making this connection, I made another.

With all this walking away from things, there has been one thing I have stayed consistent with and have not abandoned – my faith and my relationship with God.

And this second connection led me to an important question: Why can I stick to my faith but not all of the things that come with daily life?

Why did I fight them … or better yet, why did I often run from them?

Why was it that every time I was discouraged or overwhelmed, I became convinced that there must be an easier way?

Why was it that every time I become frustrated or upset, I was throwing in the towel?

Personally, I came to realize, on the other hand, that when it came to my faith, I persevered because it's just that – faith.

I have seen so many people question their faith. Even to the point of God's existence. That's a path I refuse to take. My faith tells me that God does exist, and I see it every day in myself and in the lives around me.

Period. I need no convincing. And I trust in God that I never will.

That is perseverance. Never letting anything shake us, or tempt us into taking a different path.

Our faith in God should never be dependent on feelings, fads or the opinions of the next bestselling author who has another option, or way of thinking.

No, thank you.

Whether it comes to work life, home life, family life, etc., we need to stay on the path regardless of our feelings, even when things prove difficult. Moods and feelings change every hour of the day but we must stand firm, just as we do in our loyalty to God.

With everything in life, sometimes we enjoy what we receive, and other times, we will dislike it. Can we always be grateful though?

It's our challenge to rise above these changing and sometimes negative feelings and find God's will in our circumstances. He will give us the ability to persevere through these challenges, however great or small.

How often do we look for greener grass, only to find a desert?

How often do we shift our direction because of imagined fears?

Many times we realize that the trials that troubled us were actually good for us. They helped us to see which virtues we possess or need to strengthen, so we can improve our daily lives.

I think if we can honestly admit it, our worst enemy is mostly, well – ourselves. We will often dislike the harder course of action every single time. And we will do anything we can to find a better, more pleasing option. But that is not virtuous. It is actually fear, and well, laziness.

Our imagination, our feelings, our old habits, our likes and dislikes, these will assist us only in abandoning necessary struggles and obstacles in our life, and eventually, giving up.

Learn to pray more and more to God, asking Him to help you gain more perseverance.

To stop avoiding.

To stop looking for green grass.

To stop imagining distant splendor.

What Really Matters

SEEKING THE PURPOSE

God often takes things from us for His own good reasons.

Our task is to seek the purpose.

Everyone has suffered many losses throughout their lives. Some losses were major, like the death of a loved one, sickness or heartache.

Some losses were minor, inconvenient or just plain annoying, like when I lost my sense of smell.

When I was in my late twenties I was fired abruptly from my job as the Director of Marketing for a small business in the town in which I grew up. Only one week before getting the boot, I was given an employee review, receiving high marks on everything and was even told I was an asset to the company. Yet a week later I was told I was being let go due to poor performance, to collect my things … and leave.

It was a bit of a head scratcher.

I was good at this job. I was happy at this job. And it was taken away from me.

I was mad. I was resentful. I was bitter.

But I did what anyone else would do…I looked for a new job. And after several months of searching, I found one.

A good one.

It was with a very large company, in a much larger city than my hometown. It involved lots of hard work, lots of extra hours and was accompanied by lots of travel.

It was exhausting, and I loved it.

I learned a lot and made friends and colleagues that still endure many years later.

I realize now that God knew I would never leave the job in my hometown because it felt so safe and secure. And back then safety and security were everything to me.

God also knew that I wasn't growing as a person there. So He gave me the push I needed. And there is no greater push than a heave-ho.

It turns out that the new job took me out of my safe zone, and helped me to break out of my shell. It helped me to find my voice.

And it also helped me with humility. Within a few short years, when I started thinking back to that old job in my hometown, I realized I wasn't as good as I thought I was there. Sure, I was reliable, diligent and a hard worker ... but I was also quiet, nervous and often apprehensive.

And perhaps dare I say, even though the way I was let go was done poorly, maybe in hindsight I deserved to be dismissed.

God knew this. I certainly didn't.

And His good reasons for allowing me to be fired, humiliated and suffer for months with little to no income was because He knew I needed this.

All of it.

And leaving that old job wasn't just about the job. Because, as always, God has deeper intentions in mind. Intentions that go far beyond our way of perceiving things.

Taking the new job meant I had to move away from my hometown to be closer to the new position. And this helped me to make new friends. And some of these friends helped introduce to me to the Catholic faith.

At the time, I was a die-hard Agnostic. Sure there was a God, but I had no interest in knowing Him or following His laws. Or even wanting Him in my life.

But yet, not even two years later, I was confirmed and baptized into the Catholic faith. I still look back at the amazement of it. And I thank

God every day for my faith. And for putting me into a position that finally made me seek the purpose.

His purpose.

And not only did I make new friends but some of these friends became instrumental in my life.

God took my old job from me for His own good reasons.

And my task was to seek the purpose.

And I did.

I realize now that the purpose wasn't about me working for a large company, or living in a large city. That was the just the means to help me find what I needed most. Faith in Jesus Christ.

In time I returned back to my hometown. But not as the same person. And I learned that through it all, God always knows what we need.

He knows when we should have more and He knows when we should have less.

He knows when to take us out of our comfort zone, even if it's very hard.

And ultimately, He knows what is good for our soul. And it's our task to recognize and answer His call.

When you realize (and accept) that God is running the show, it's hard to become mad, or resentful or even bitter ... because when we leave our life in His hands, we find it much easier to avoid all the negative feelings of loss or denial and replace them with gratitude and hope.

So often in life we're tempted to think that other people have more than we do – that they are better off than us or that they are treated better than us.

But as we try to grow in a genuine union with God, we are able to think and see things more clearly and correctly.

It's not easy. But if we keep trying and are diligent in our efforts, we are able to find more peace and even gratitude when life seems dark and unbearable. So, whether we're successful or have failed or we're experiencing joy or sorrow, as long as our only wish is to please and honor God in our every thought, word and deed …

We will be OK. More than OK.

Whether we experience the loss of a job, a loved one, a fortune or even our sense of smell, He is with us.

Because you'll realize that God is taking care of you at every moment and has His good reasons for everything that happens in your life. You just need only keep your eyes on Him and let Him take control.

And in the end, when you meet God face-to-face, you'll fully realize just how wise and loving He was in His care of you.

Seek the purpose. You'll be glad you did.

THE TRUE MEASURE OF SUCCESS

Many people in life strive for success. Whether it be in their education, career or in the extra-curricular activities they pursue.

For me, success has never really been something that I believed was very important.

Now, that may seem odd. I mean, what kind of person doesn't want to be successful?

But actually, truth be told, I am interested in being successful. Just not the world's version of it.

I think the problem I have with 'success' is how it's normally defined. Is success becoming famous, wealthy, creating a big moneymaking business or coming up with an idea that people can't live without?

Perhaps. But again, it depends on how you define success.

If all you're striving for is money, a successful business or fame … will you keep your dignity to achieve it? Will you help to improve the lives of others?

Will you please God?

And at what cost? For 'success'?

One thing is certain. Whatever your definition of success is, it's something you're looking for, something that exists in the future. It's based on your desire to achieve something for yourself due to your feelings that you're not where you want to be. Worldly people seek to define their success from the esteem and praise from one another. Success is often based on status and admiration.

At best it's vain. And it's also extremely subjective.

Human glory, worldly honor, and earthly possessions – these are all empty and meaningless when compared to the love, honor and glory of God. True greatness and success is not in a person who is satisfied with himself. It is only in those servants in whom God is well-pleased. (Matt. 25:23)

God will never gauge our merits or success by our knowledge, education, wealth, status, or position among others. But God will measure our success by our self-sacrifice, humility and charity towards others.

God knows when we think and rely too much on ourselves, rather than seeking His will. He knows when we give honor and glory to ourselves, rather than honoring and glorifying Him.

Don't get me wrong, I'm not saying that a good education, a good work position or owning your own company is a bad thing. But it is a bad thing if your motivation is based in wanting or desiring admiration from others.

God alone is to be worshiped. Not us. If we love God in all things, we will praise His Name, not ours. We will esteem and honor God's Will, not our own estimation of personal success and accomplishments. In the end, true success can only be measured in one way.

Success is defined in finding joy, love, honor and glory in God. And if you find your success and accomplishment in God, and in God alone, you have found the greatest level of success ever possible.

THE POWER OF GOODBYE

Many times in life, we move on. And we say goodbye.

A goodbye to a lifestyle, employment, location, or even a goodbye to the people or things we have in close proximity to our lives.

And it's definitely not always easy.

As a means in helping ourselves to maintain a strong faith, we must often learn to abandon many aspects of the world, even though we must continue to live in it.

We should also strive to realize more and more that God must be the first and highest desire of our soul because God is goodness. And without a just and perfect God to lead us … we're headed for trouble. And by taking a look at the world and its current list of elephantine-sized problems, it also doesn't take a rocket scientist to realize – we're already there.

And I'm not just talking about politics, world leaders and all of the social and moral issues of today. This also applies to things on a much less-grand scale.

Anything that removes God as our highest priority should be re-evaluated.

Life is full of distractions and attachments. And when you start to remove those distractions and attachments that are either unhealthy or even just excessively time-consuming, and instead give that time and focus to God and in helping your neighbor, you will naturally start to think more clearly and act more in accordance to God's Will in all matters.

Most of life's struggles, from frustrations to anxiety, from anger to sadness, from grief to worry, all tend to stem from the same thing …

The struggles come from being too tightly attached to something, or someone, or even ourselves, instead of being attached to God.

Instead of relying on God.

Not giving God the attention He deserves.

And when we start to properly recognize these distractions and attachments and are able to say goodbye to them, amazing things start to happen, because there is power in saying, "Goodbye," to what is often around us.

Goodbyes force us to start over.

Goodbyes remind us that nothing in this world lasts forever.

Goodbyes can stop us from continuing bad habits.

Goodbyes can help us to remove who or what is toxic or unhealthy from our lives.

Goodbyes can prompt us to find true meaning in our lives.

And goodbyes can often bring new hellos.

When we are ready to say goodbye to distractions, habits and even unhealthy relationships, we are ready to embrace new opportunities, new people and a deeper relationship with God.

And it's then that many of our goodbyes will make more sense to us and we will be glad that we turned that page, moving on to new or stronger chapters in our life.

To know, love and trust God.

DETERMINATION

Saying you want something is one thing but actually doing something about it is very different. We prove what we desire most by our actions, not by our words. Where our treasure is – there will our heart be also.

We see this and experience it all the time, in others and in our own lives.

And since finding my faith, I can't help but recognize the determination that each of us needs to live the type of life that God wants and expects from each of us.

We want to be forgiving but how often do we continue to hold grudges? We want to be more patient but do we truly make the changes in our thoughts and actions to demonstrate patience? We want to start being more charitable but do we avoid people who call on us for help? We desire to have more gratitude for what we have but how often do we continue to want more instead of appreciating what we already have?

Or how about this one? We desire to love God with our whole heart and soul but how often do we find reasons to not include Him in our lives, whether consciously or unconsciously?

How often is what we say we want different from what we actually pursue? Saying you want something is one thing, doing something about it is very different. We prove what we desire most by our actions, not by our words. Yes, it was worth repeating!

We should ask ourselves: Am I taking the necessary steps to grow closer in my relationship with God? A true relationship? Am I taking the steps to overcome my defects and let God turn them into virtues? And strive for continual determination?

We have to keep going and never give up – no matter how many times we fall and even if we fall hard. We cannot give up. God loves us and is merciful.

A desire to be a better person for God, without the necessary spiritual work to become that better person ... is just wishful thinking.

It will take some work on our part.

Actions.

Strength.

Determination.

YOUR LAST DAYS

Everyone's life on this earth is finite. And that fact is astounding.

Everyone has their final days ahead of them but how many of us really put much time into preparing for them? How many of us truly consider just how short our lives really are? How many of us reflect on how little time we have to live our life in a way that is more deep and meaningful?

Imagine if you only had a month left to live. How would you spend your last days? One more month and then you will die.

Would your focus be on traveling?

Would you spend it learning about various topics as much as you can?

Would you attempt to create a legacy for yourself by doing something that will help to ensure you're remembered long after you're gone?

Any of those choices, or a combination of them, might seem like a worthwhile way to spend that month.

But by whose standards?

You can argue that any of the activities I listed are worthwhile, and that's fine — the point is to decide what's worthy of your final month of life on this earth.

Is parachuting out of a plane the final swan song of your life?

Is booking a trip to India going to give you more peace on your deathbed?

I admit, both sound interesting and maybe even fun. Well, less the hurling yourself hundreds of feet to the ground part. I'll pass on that.

But perhaps we need to have the courage to make a choice that is deeper.

A choice that, in my estimation, is essential.

A choice that will help us to grow closer to God.

Grow closer to God? Alan, are you nuts? I would go skydiving!

Think about it, though. All of the moments in our lives are not just fleeting and precious; they are also very limited.

We were put on this Earth by God, to know and love Him, so that we can be with Him forever.

And when God puts an inevitable storm in our path, a storm which ends up taking us from this Earth, we have to know how to hold firm in the storm – not by holding on to whatever superficial things we can find for as long as we can find them – whether it be vacations, skydiving or even by giving into our lower nature through indulging in vice … but instead by trusting that the one Person who matters most in this world will never let go of us.

And in return, we must never let go of Him.

That's what perfect love is.

Perfect love casts out all fear and replaces it with hope.

So, make a choice. Decide what you'll squeeze into those final precious days.

Personally, I hope I find the strength and the courage to spend my final moments in deep prayer and reflection, growing closer and closer to God. Asking forgiveness from those I have offended and sincerely, from the bottom of my heart, forgiving others for anything they may have done to me in the past. True repentance brings true freedom.

Jesus gave his life for us all. And at the end of our lives, we commend our spirit back to Him.

But actually, why wait until our dying days to give ourselves over to prayer and reflection?

Instead, why not spend every day as if it is our last?

Because in reality, tomorrow may very well be your last day on Earth. It may even be today.

Don't waste your life.

It goes so quickly.

And knowing the day, month or year of your death, may be a gift you won't receive.

Live for God today. So you can spend an eternity with Him forever.

We can do this. Together. With God by our side.

Never give up on your quest for virtue.

CONCLUSION

I wrote these articles and this book with the express intention to inspire and challenge you. I hope you have read this book, not only with your head, but with your heart.

And reading this book should be just the beginning of your journey. To live a life that is focused and centered on Our Lord, you will need prayer, perspective, time for growth, a sincere love for God, and a willingness to change for the better.

With that said, please be patient with yourself and also with others. An honest attempt to grow in virtue will most certainly never be easy. Failure is part of life, so knowing that, don't give up when it happens – keep moving forward.

Lastly, please join me and other readers on the blog by going to growinvirtue.com to share your thoughts and experiences.

Prayers and blessings for your journey to union with God.

Alan Scott

ACKNOWLEDGMENTS

I have gained so much from the help and support of others in creating both this book, and the Grow in Virtue website. I am grateful for the sharing, opinions, education, insights, editing, and advice that have been provided to me from my friends, family and colleagues.

A special thank you to Matthew Sheffield, Summer Crosbie, Jessica Hooper, Donna Sheffield, Susan Spalding, Jason Himmelright, Margaret Himmelright, Kristi McCarty, Thorsten Thurner, Cathy Cowans, Bernadette Sheffield, Mary Stronsider, Debby Weber, Sharon Cooper, Jane Eiler, Tom Gilson, Michael J. Lichens, Tony Agnesi, Rose Folsom, Reshma Thomas, Father Edward Looney, Father Robert Maro, Denise Renner, Sheena Lukose, and all of the wonderful readers who have embraced and supported the topic of virtue.

ABOUT THE AUTHOR

 Alan Scott is a writer and designer residing in Virginia. A former Agnostic, he converted to the Catholic faith in 2004. In 2014 he started his blog GrowInVirtue.com, which focuses on growing in holiness, by attempting to live a life more simple and virtuous, a life that is lived for God. When he's not writing or designing, you'll find him, hands dirty, in his garden.

To continue reading new articles from
Alan Scott about faith and virtue, please visit:

www.GrowInVirtue.com

Made in the USA
Columbia, SC
08 September 2017